The Home Reader

A Paranormal Journey

CELINA MYERS

;

A Portion of your purchase of this book will be
donated to mental health services in Woodstock
Ontario. Our little town has suffered a large amount
of teen suicide recently. A semi colon is used when
a writer chooses to pause instead of ending a
sentence. If you are reading this and find yourself in
a dark place. Please reach out, even to me.
Your story is not supposed to end yet.

Taken and Based On True Events.......

All names and locations have been changed to protect those involved.

The Home Reader
A Paranormal Journey

I dedicate this book to my dear friend Rodney Tranter
and my husband Adam Myers.

For these
two men I am forever grateful.
Their kindness has been such an inspiration.
The world needs more people like them.

THE BEGINNING

Within the years of our lives, we are
often lost in the journey to find ourselves. We
search and explore for our spirits to be flushed
out by adults telling us who we are to be. We
are so often told what we are, who we are, and
what we see, that we forget who we have
become. Despite a constant wave of people
applauding (or hating) us for who we may

project, there is always a moment in our lives that we realize we are different.

The first time I realized that I - Celina Myers - was different was as a small child. It seemed to be something that my parents had known for years, although that could be dismissed as a parent's tendency to see their child as special. On that particular day, I had a warm feeling of excitement because I was going to my friend Tessa's house to stay the night.

Once I arrived, my six-year-old self devoured my surroundings with an energetic fever of curiosity. Even though Tessa was familiar to me, her routines and little details of her life were foreign and unfamiliar. Why didn't she place her stuffed animals like a shield around her bed? How was she able to sleep with the lights off? The more I explored her home, the higher my questions piled. This was when I began to suspect that perhaps my life was less than normal.

At my own home, the bed had to be in the middle of the room against the north wall. Each and every night to this day, I would sleep with my sheets tucked as high as possible, the light on. No matter the heat in the room, I would not allow even one foot to slide out of the sheets. No matter how uncomfortable it felt I had to sleep on my side facing the doors, not to mention that all of my stuffed animals had to be arranged just right.

All of these actions made me feel comfortable – if not physically, then at least emotionally. These were my defences against the things I feared. At six years old, I knew that there were people in my walls. Sometimes it would be a little girl who would poke me when I slept. Other times it would be other spirits. This was not something others would understand. Regardless, this was my reality.

The wall of stuffed animals blocked my eyes as I looked over the side of the bed. They created a barrier high enough to block the eerie gaze of people that would emerge from the two-foot strip of wall between my closets. As I grew older and more conscious of the world around me, I realized that these things were not normal and with that realization, my exceptionality was smothered by conformity. In fact, that sleepover at Tessa's house sparked a series of realizations that I was different. My distinct talent started to fade, and like so many others, I became addicted to the disguise of being 'normal'.

A large part of my identity was formed in my family home. My parents had purchased a newly-built Dutch colonial house in 1990. It had been built barely six months earlier, and as soon as my parents laid eyes on it, they were sold.

They were lucky, too. The market had changed drastically, allowing them to sell the semi they had made their own for the past decade to purchase something better. They didn't want to simply buy a house; they had the intention of settling into a home.

They dreamed of a house on a large street with an abundance of joyful neighbourhood kids scurrying about. My mom was five months pregnant with me so there was an urgency to take advantage of the situation while they could. The family who had built the home was hesitant to leave their dream home, however my parents made it work.

One thing that didn't work in their favour was the supernatural. The circumstances before my birth and the reoccurrence of bizarre - and sometimes unexplainable - things over the course of my life have led me to believe in the existence of something more.

Shortly after Mom and Dad settled into the house and just before my birth, small dresser drawers and picture frames would be moved or pulled out from the walls as if someone was playing a trick on my parents.

Other little things started to happen. Chiming musical sounds filled the house at odd hours of the day, which my mother dismissed as the sounds of wind chimes in the summer breeze. These chimes continued to fill the house daily, but she assumed that as the colder weather approached, the sound would be smothered by the shut windows and humming furnace.

The first cold day of October arrived. The windows were shut firmly, rendering the house silent. My mother was folding laundry on her bed when, out of the dead silence, came soft chime like music. Looking over her shoulder at the door, she remembered that the windows were shut so there could be no residual noise coming from outside. The furnace was also off.

This time the music was clearer and sharper, and its sound became that soft kind of melody that leaks from a music box. My mother made her way towards the noise. Navigating the new house was somewhat difficult. The house was large and when you turned out of the master bedroom you entered a hallway that had a large open expanse stretching from the first floor to the second. The stairs came up on the left side and an oversized chandelier hung in the middle. From the floor to the celling was a space of nearly thirty feet.

She slipped down the stairs quietly, trying not to make a sound. At the end of this hallway there was an eat-in kitchen, but before that were short hallways on each side, making a T-shaped intersection. One of those halls led to a family room while the other led to the basement, living room, and dining room.

My mother turned down the hall to the right and into the family room, but quickly realized the sound didn't originate from there. She looked back through the door and stared into the opposite hallway. The space in front of the basement door is what held her attention. It was as if dust was catching in the light, just like it does in front of a sunny window on a bright day. However, the difference here was that there was no light. It was the evening and the particles of dust were ten times that of a normal speck.

That wasn't the only odd occurrence, either. A few months after I was born, my dad was carrying me down the open large front hallway. As he looked down at my small cherub face, he noticed my eyes were following something erratically. Glancing up, he saw a ball of light bouncing from wall to wall and changing size and speed. He wasn't sure how to respond to this so he just went into the living room and tried to forget.

A few months later my parents had no choice but to agree that something unnatural was going on in their new home. It was the middle of the night when my mom heard the soft coos of a baby beside her bed. My dear mother turned on her bedside lamp, only to see me on the floor beside her bed. I'd only just learned how to crawl, and there was no way I could have pulled myself out of the crib. Somehow, someone or something had taken me out of my crib and I crawled my way to my parent's room.

After that night, things quieted down for a couple years, and the memory of those bizarre happenings settled themselves into the recesses of my parents' minds.

Life settled into a mundane sort of rhythm. My father worked the afternoon shift every two weeks. He came home late one night and was making his way up the stairs when he suddenly heard my three-year-old voice talking in my bedroom. He popped open the door and saw me sitting straight up in bed. I turned my head and silently looked at him. "Who are you talking to?" he said. "The people in my wall," I replied.

Instead of investigating my father had a "nope" moment. He promptly closed the door and didn't tell me about this incident until I was twenty-three years old. Learning that story was a huge part of why I am writing this now. I thought the people from my walls were just a figment of my creative imagination, but they turned out to be something more.

A few nights later, everything changed. For months I had been talking of a little girl named Mary. She was the one who would poke me in bed if my walls of stuffed animals were not in place. She was the one who would play pranks, for which I would be blamed.

One evening, my mother was readying herself for a small errand run. She prepped the stroller, the diaper bag, and all the stuff typical of overfilled baby care packs that new mothers lugged around. As she prepared, she heard a noise behind her. Turning around, she saw as clear as day and as solid as you or I, a child standing under the kitchen table. The girl was about 4 years old, wore a white nightgown that reached her knees, and sported a pageboy hair cut.

She could pass off all of her other experiences as some kind of "coincidence" or "mistake"- maybe a "trick of the light" - but this was a little girl under her table. My mother realized that all the events that had happened had seemed prankish and childish, something that a little girl might do. As my mother watched, the girl disappeared into thin air.

Thinking back to my talk of a little girl, Mom called a family friend who was also the local historian. His family had been one of the founders of our little town.

On the Saturday before the historian came, my parents took me to the Western Fair in London, Ontario. It was the first time I'd been to such a magical place. I got a large red balloon as a souvenir to take home. As soon as we walked in the front door, I lost hold of the balloon and it floated right up into the large open space in the front hallway. There was absolutely no way of getting it down, though my mom thought it would make its way back to the first floor as the helium broke down.

That evening she awoke. Somehow, perhaps with the current of the air conditioner, the balloon had made its way into her room. That was a perfectly logical explanation but for the fact that the balloon landed directly on top of her face. She reached for the bedside lamp and flicked the switch. Sitting up, she pushed the balloon away with enough force to send it across the room, but the balloon quickly bounced back. There was resistance at the end of the string...like something was holding it in place.

She got up abruptly in a panic and ripped the balloon from the unseen hands, but the tension was gone. She then shut the balloon in her closet and somehow fell back asleep.

The next day, the same kitchen table the little girl has been standing under was covered from corner to corner with old blueprints and land maps. The historian had a general idea of what had been on the land before the house was built, and went over the brief history of the property.

In the late 1800's, a small farmhouse sat directly where our large home now resided. It was the home of the Nellis family, who owned dozens of surrounding acres and were influential to the city of Woodstock. They had given away land for a farmer's market on Nellis street and also donated land for a cemetery - where you can now find their own plots - on Vansittart Avenue.

Since they were a prominent family, the historian had many files and even some pictures of the family. The first picture the historian brought out of the folder to show my mother was of the large family. As she looked over the photo, an expression of shock and disbelief took over my mother's features. She pointed at one of the little girls sitting cross-legged; it was the little girl that she saw under the table in our kitchen! The historian said her name was Mary Agnes Nellis. Mary, along with one of her sisters, had died as a child of scarlet fever in that home in the 1800's.

Upon learning this information, my mother felt she didn't have to fear the strange things that happened. These unsettling events were just caused by a little girl stuck somewhere between the living and the dead. It seemed that when we knew and accepted who she was, the occurrences began to fade. Things still happened, but they were slower and weaker, and they had completed stopped by the time I was 7 years old. Well, until I hit puberty.

As a pre-teen, I felt like I couldn't tell anyone about the things I was starting to see, hear, feel and smell. At such a tender age, I already knew how this news would be received. Confessing that I was hearing voices and seeing things would condemn me socially.

Every day I was seeing more and more. Each and every day I was seeing something different. I doubted myself until I could doubt no more. It became a cycle of disbelief and discomfort with my distinct reality. From hearing things at home to seeing things in the grocery store, every day was different.

One day I was at school in the change room getting ready for gym class when a man suddenly appeared out of nowhere. Though I was startled and frightened to see a man in the girls' change room, I didn't call out because it didn't seem like anyone else saw him. I would look crazy, even though I knew I wasn't. It was a difficult situation.

The man continuously paced. He walked seven feet forward, seven feet back. Back and forth, back and forth, like he was engrossed in thought. Suddenly I noticed that from the torso down, his body was submerged in the ground. That's when I was convinced that what I was seeing was not normal.

His curly, dark hair was shoulder length, he had a beard, and he wore a brown overcoat. His eyes were glazed and he held his hand over his mouth, completely unaware of the world around him. Stunned, curiosity overruled fear of ridicule, and I decided to see if anyone else was seeing this strange sight. I looked over at two other girls in the change room.

"Hey," I tentatively called. The shorter of the two girls looked over.

"Hi, how are you?" she said. The other girl just continued to fold her shorts into her gym bag.

"Good," I said. "Um...I don't know how to ask this...but did you see a guy in here?"

The other girl looked up sharply from her gym bag and clutched her towel to her chest in panic. The shorter girl looked quizzically at her friend and then at me.

"No, I don't think so. Probably was a shadow." She shrugged.

I sighed. They didn't see him. The spirit continued on its journey to and fro. He didn't notice any of us. People walked through him, but his features and his pacing never changed. I exited the change room in a furor of fright. I was seeing things others could not, and I needed to figure out what was happening to me.

For the remainder of my schooling days I changed in the bathroom instead of the change room. It wasn't until I was older that I learned that what I had seen was a perfect display of residual energy.

Another day in class, I was copying a note from the chalkboard when I noticed a shadow starting to bend over me. I felt the warm exhale of breath on my shoulder and initially thought nothing of it, thinking a student was simply walking behind my desk. The young student teacher assigned to our class continued to preach knowledge at the front of the room.

Another ten minutes passed before I suddenly felt lingering eyes upon my back. The warm breath became more pronounced. Heavier. Hotter. Deeper. With a quick glance over my shoulder, I saw no one was there. My heart quickened. My eyes darted across the room and searched frantically for the source of the air.

It appeared that everything was in order. My teacher was sitting at her desk to the left of me and the student teacher was at a table directly to the side. It could be a student pranking me, I thought to myself. I needed to double check without being called out for fidgeting, or being sent to the hall. Keeping my eyes down, I slowly turned my head to the right, all the while praying that this was just a strange mouth-breathing student and not something else.

I looked to the floor first and saw a pair of pink patent leather shoes. My gaze traveled up the nylon-covered legs to find a very old, tiny woman dressed completely in pink from head to toe, all the way down to her pink painted nails. I focused on her happy-looking wrinkled face, completely unsure if this was a real person or 'one of them'.

"Hello," she croaked out of her pink lipstick-stained lips. The prudish wrinkles of her face curved into a wide toothless smile, the kind that makes you feel bubbly on the inside.

Though I knew I might later regret it, I had to reply. In that moment, I was unconcerned with how it would look to my classmates. "Hi," I said quietly.

A flutter of surprise passed over the woman's face. She looked more shocked then I felt. "You can hear me then?" The words came out of her mouth in a very strange tone. It sounded warped and distant as if someone was speaking through a tube from a mile away. It was like the notes and chords of her voice were melting into one another in a way that made the words barely audible.

I nodded my head and looked around at everyone, hoping that this was somehow a real person, but no one around me had noticed her presence. I knew that this pink lady really stuck out. If she was real, everyone would be staring and laughing.

For most of my teen years, I had decided to just keep the things to myself. I found if I kept my mind busy and repeated the mantra "it's not real if you don't want it to be," things would stay a lot quieter at school. (Unfortunately, the mantra only seemed to work at school. Nights and the odd apparition like this were a different game.) As I stared at the woman, I began repeating my mantra to myself, but she wasn't disappearing. As a matter of fact, the happy look that had come to her face was quickly fading into a deep frown.

I felt guilty, but the new discovery that "these people" could actually see and talk to me was so overwhelming that I didn't know how to react. I usually just watched their lives unfold. Sometimes I would catch one looking right at me, but no one had uttered so much as a single word directly to me.

As much as I wanted the pink lady to disappear, I knew there was more to this situation. Her arm rose, and I turned to follow the direction of her stumpy finger. She was pointing to the young student teacher. I looked back at the pink lady, and as her mouth slowly opened, her breath filled my face.

"I need you to tell her to take the trip, and that I have Skittles with me." Her arm slowly lowered back to her side and a smile crossed her face. She walked noiselessly behind me and followed the back wall that was plastered with our artwork before effortlessly passing through the closed classroom door.

It took me three days to finally come up with the nerve to approach the student teacher. It was when I saw her alone in the corner of the courtyard at recess that I decided to approach. I knew the best way to to this was to just spill it all out fast, before she had a chance to interrupt.

I walked up to her and quickly relayed to her the conversation that had been haunting me. The teacher's cheeks turned pink and warm droplets of tears collected at the corner of her eyes. She explained that the pink lady was her great-grandmother, then started to sob. It had been seven long years since her great-grandmother was laid to rest, but their bond had been extremely close. She had never connected with any other relative that way. She told me how the clothing I described was exactly what her great-grandmother had been wearing when she passed. "Skittles" was a reference to the teacher's 11-year-old Siamese cat that had passed only two weeks prior. The trip the pink lady had mentioned was a gift from the student teacher's boyfriend, but she had always been scared of planes, so was unsure whether or not she wanted to go.

I was blown away that what I saw had made any sense to her, let alone be verified to be true. There was no way I could have known anything about her life.

Oddly enough, I was overcome with relief. Finally, I was able to tell someone the things that were going on. My student teacher assured me that I wasn't sick, that sometimes people are just born different with what she called "gifts." She said there were ways to control them if I wanted to, and also ways to shut them off.

The following week she brought me a book that discussed just that. I can't start to explain how much that teacher did for me, and how much she impacted my future by just telling me there was nothing to fear.

My teen years were full of difficulties and strife. When I was twelve, my mother's multiple sclerosis reared its ugly head. Life was full of hospital visits. These visits would often be accented with urgency, some of which came from my deteriorating relationship with my father.

Engrossed in stress and alienation, anger blocked out whatever comfort I might have felt.

I'd hear small fragmented sentences from disembodied voices floating about as I walked down the hospitals halls.

I randomly saw ghosts walking around my house or standing in the middle of my street in clothing from the 1980's. I started to resonate with them. In some ways they looked lost, their eyes glazed over as they relived their best and worst memories in their minds. It seemed that as soon as I forgot about them, something else would happen to assure me that this was not something that would just fade with age.

It wasn't until a few years later that I was really able to get a handle on exactly what I was experiencing.

At the tender age of fifteen, after changing high schools twice, not making friends and being picked on so violently that the police had to be called several times, I decided being alive was too painful. People didn't take kindly to girls who dressed only in black and changed schools twice in her first semester of grade 9. I found myself leaving the public high school and transferring to a catholic school. I was hoping that the plaid uniforms would help me blend into my surroundings; regrettably, that wasn't the case. When I tried to end my life, I instead ended up at the Woodstock General Hospital.

I quickly became a staple in the psychiatric wing of our local hospital, making friends with all the nurses and the other teen girls like me who had attempted suicide. Some had swallowed all the prescription drugs they could find; others had made a jump that they thought would land them anywhere but here.

Being only 15, I was not allowed to join in with the group counselling, so I spent my days sitting on the couch in the common room. I didn't opt for the TV and decided to just invest my time in staring at my surroundings. It was a reminder of the outside world.

The beige room was sizable like the rest of the hospital, its windows blocked by vast old trees and grated with cast iron bars to prevent us from further attempts at ending our lives. The common room sat at the end of the wings hall, letting its inhabitants watch the day's activities.

I realized that if I focused really hard on one spot of the chipping beige paint for a few minutes, the world would start to change around me. The spot would get all fuzzy around the edges, and in my mind I would see the wing of the hospital in another time. Sometimes it would just be one side of the hall or just for a few seconds, but the longer I worked at it, the clearer it became.

On one particular day, I stared at a 40-year-old woman who had been admitted for the past two months. She was here because her depression had led her to swallow all of her and her daughter's anti-depressants. We always seemed to be in the common room at the same time. That day, she was working on a portrait at one of the three tables to the left of me. My concentration broke when she asked, "What exactly are you doing?" She said it patiently, and I knew that she had caught on to my strangeness.

I explained that I had just seen the hallway in another light as if it was very early morning. I told her how a very tiny man in a Boston Bruin's sweater had come out of the third room on the left dragging a very oversized teddy bear. I laughed when mentioning it, because I knew that I sounded 100% insane.

"Well, that's Randy, he left a week before you came." I sat there in confusion, perplexed by the fact that she wasn't shocked by my revelation.

After coming to the conclusion that what I saw was real and not an illness, I learned to trust myself. I learned that I needed to trust what I did and didn't see. I couldn't let other people gaslight me. I explained my experiences to the doctor, and how the people the spirits were reaching out to had validated the experiences. He seemed more impressed then anything, and after our conversations, he didn't think I had any kind of schizophrenia whatsoever. The doctor said that I was there because I was suffering from a heavy depression in the first place, not because of the ghosts.

The ward was a fantastic place to practice my "gift," as it was a controlled environment. There was lots of residual energy in a place like the psychiatric wing. People came here during the hardest times of their lives, so there were large memories expressed and left behind. It was around this time that I started to comprehend that I wasn't only seeing "dead people."

I quickly learned that 90% of the time I was seeing memories, not lost souls. Don't get me wrong - I have seen a *lot* of the ghostly variety. The ghosts are what I can't control to this day. The spirits that I see are always solid as you or me. I don't choose to see them or have the ability to call on them. They don't always speak to me, either; most of the time they don't notice anything around them. They are so deep in thought it seems like they are reliving unfinished business. Only sometimes do they search me out, or notice me noticing them.

During my stay in the hospital I had a lot of time to think, but I never could have imagined how much my life would revolve around this so-called "gift," and how every situation I put myself in would be affected. It is a truly beautiful thing at times, but also a curse at other times. I don't like to think of what I do as a gift; it's just who I am. I feel most people could tap into abilities like this if they really work at it. I was just born a bit better at it, just like how some people seem to be naturals at math.

I spent the next few years being a fun party trick, delivering messages to people that I received from random spirits along the way. I am 25 years old now, and in the past decade my gifts have grown and been studied by many. I have taken part in some high-scale investigations and worked with some of the top parapsychologists and demonologists.

I have traveled a lot of North America to help people. Every day I am learning more and more. I feel I am extremely lucky, and in the end, I wouldn't want things any other way.

I only have one regret. I always worked under pseudonyms and tried to keep what I did separate from my personal life. I held such a fear of certain people finding out; for instance, that employers wouldn't like what they could learn about me on the Internet. I respect famous parapsychologists like Ed and Lorrain

Warren, but I couldn't live life in the spotlight, to take on all that responsibility. Most people working in the paranormal field know that a lot of eccentric people are drawn to the unknown. I didn't want people to assume I'm something that I'm not. I needed to learn to shed the terrible ego I was afraid of.

It wasn't until I joined a local paranormal team that I found myself explaining what I did over and over. Then came the worst: another paranormal team native to the area decided to blast our paranormal team.

It was as if this group had set out to destroy all of us personally, because we had come onto their "turf." To this day, that experience is the most disrespected and personally attacked I have ever felt. I could have told that group about the life I lived, the places I had been and the people I had worked with, but I couldn't expect them listen to anything, so I tried to not acknowledge them.

In that moment, I decided to change how I went about everything. The secrecy I came to love and use as a protective blanket was now working against me. I needed my name out there so I could be taken seriously for who I am. I needed to treat *myself* with respect and embrace who I really am.

At 25, I wasn't sure what I wanted to do with the rest of my life. I didn't want the "paranormal" to taint anything I had planned. So much of my life had been unwillingly submerged in the paranormal I didn't think that was who I wanted to be.

I was wrong.

I didn't realize that I needed to learn to accept what was right in front of me.

I might have played with the idea before, but the truth is that this is my life. It's who I am, and who I will always be. I don't know what my future holds, but I can only hope sharing my experiences and thoughts will only open more doors.

This book is a collection of my experiences, the investigations I have been called into, and my thoughts on what I think comes next.

I hope you enjoy.

Celina Myers
The host of "The Haunted Estate Podcast"
www.TheHauntedEstate.com

THE HUNTSVILLE ESTATE

It was July, and the sun was beaming down and heating the roads to Huntsville, a beautiful area nestled in the heart of the wilderness of Northern Ontario. This stunning town had a nest of secrets waiting for me. As I made my first trip up to this quaint place, I recalled the events that drew me out of the comfort of my home.

It had been a startling beginning to the morning. I jolted awake to a five a.m. phone call, which I groggily answered despite the unrecognized number.

The voice on the other end of the line belonged to a man who was speaking at break neck speed, racing into an introduction before I'd even said hello. The urgency in his voice was palpable, so I took hold of the conversation.

"Hello! Hello!" I tried to cut into the rapid stream of speech. "Please slow down so I can understand you." The man paused and exhaled. "I'm sorry, it's just that I've been up all night trying to find help."

"Alright, how about we start with a name?" I suggested as his breathing slowed. Careful not to disturb my slumbering spouse, I reached over to grab a notepad from my desk to record some details.

"My name is Frank and I've...I've experienced some things I can't explain."

Frank's voice had a noticeable quiver. "I thought you might be able to help me because I found you on the web and lurked you until I found your contact info."

"Nice to meet you, Frank." I had gotten enough calls like this over the years to know that sound he had in his voice. It was something that I couldn't possibly ignore. Frank began to explain that he and his wife had inherited a home that had sat empty in the back country. At that point, I stopped him from saying any more. I needed to enter the house as a blank slate. I couldn't know anything that could tamper with my subconscious when I investigated the scene. The house would tell me its own story once I got there.

Now, recalling the urgency of Frank's call, I continued on my drive through the serene countryside. Adjusting my stereo and sunglasses, I took in the fresh northern air and radiant roadside greenery. I soon arrived at the property, but there was still quite a trek to the house itself. The lane way was more suited for an ATV then a regular car, but I made it up the drive nonetheless. I had expected it to be more run down, dilapidated, or at least missing a few bricks. However, everything down to the front porch was pristine. It was as if the porch's paint had been redone yesterday.

Once I laid eyes on the house, I decided very quickly that "residence" was not the right word for this monstrosity. I later learned that Frank and his wife had thought the exact same as me.

Frank and his wife Susan got up from their porch chairs as soon as they saw my car. At first glance, I could see the navy bags of weariness under their eyes and how their bodies leaned together for support. Frank grabbed the bannister as his wife rushed to the car. Susan took my hands as soon I stepped out.

She frantically explained to me that the previous night was the first night they had spent back in the house after staying for several nights at a hotel. They woke at 2.14 a.m. to every window in the house open. All the screens had been popped out and laid on the surrounding lawn. After this, they were unable to sleep and spent the rest of the evening hyper aware on a caffeine binge.

Before we entered the house I took a few minutes to explain to them what I did; that is, I saw memories. While I might not be able to expel the problem, I hoped I could point them in the direction of an explanation.

I also told them that I had set up an investigation with a local paranormal team for later in the evening to assist in ridding the home of anything otherworldly. When I'd talked to the team earlier, I could tell that they were serious about their work. I can never stress enough that you should be very cautious of what I call "backyard ghost hunters" - some can cause much more trouble then what its worth. I can't begin to tell you the amount of cases I have been to that worsened after some camera happy people taunted the unknown. After a long telephone call I was happy with them as my assisting team for the evening.

With that bit of business concluded, Frank and Susan invited me into their home. When I first walked into the huge house I was taken aback. It was as if I had stepped into an extravagant time capsule. Feeling the old-century energy coursing in the bones of the building, I began my work.

I was far from home, so I didn't have one of my usual friends available to record my observations. Instead, I handed my index cards to Susan and asked her to write what I was about to dictate out loud. I told her to use a different card for each room and not to speak to me until I was finished. I wouldn't be able to really hear her anyway.

    We started in the front living room, which was to the left of the entrance. I took my spot on the closest couch. Focusing my eyes on a blank spot on the wall, I waited for my gift to take over.

    I am sure to say what I see and sense out loud for Susan's benefit. It starts with the sparkles that creep into the corners of my eyes, the whole house getting brighter and lighter as if the sun is illuminating all of its dark corners. The air becomes fresh with the sounds of loud birds and I begin to smell fresh-baking bread. The furniture looks plusher and younger as if new. Barely any of the décor is different, but the walls are a different color.

    My attention is drawn to the fireplace at the left side of the room. There stands a stern woman with both her hands braced against the mantel, her head down as if deep in thought. I walk to her and stand beside her. In front of her on the mantel are old dried flowers tied in a bouquet, a wooden deer, and three opaque pink glass roses. Her blue dress is long and done up to the neck, its hem grazing the floor. It's a dress I would find far too warm for comfort on this hot summer day. I next take notice of the unscreened, open windows.

The woman looks in my direction. She can't see me, of course - they almost never can. She takes her hands and presses her hair up, smoothing it along her head into its tight brown bun. I take notice of her large brown beauty mark and a noticeable scar that runs from the side of her left eye to her jaw line.

From this room I move into the kitchen. In the kitchen, I see and sense nothing, but now catch an overwhelming scent of the baking bread I'd smelled earlier. I follow the hallway into the room with the large dining table, then into the adjoining room that houses more chairs and couches. In front of me is a large desk and huge bay window.

At first I don't see him. His pallor matches the long deep table. He's a young man and stands perfectly still. In the same moment that I notice him, he is gone. I turn to find him standing at the bay window. He seems to be staring at something far away, all his focus and emotion going into the glance. Squinting, I see a strapping man digging about half a kilometre out in an area that today is hidden by brush and trees. As I realize that he is digging a grave, my concentration wavers, and I almost miss that the young man from the window is gliding away from me. He squats beside a buffet and tucks something underneath the dark wood.

He stands, wipes his hands on his brown trousers, and heads for the toy-littered stairs. I follow. Amongst the toys, there's a doll made from a corncob, which his lanky legs graze over as he ascends the staircase. At the top, he takes the first right into a bedroom, where he moves a picture above the master bed to reveal a hole in the wall. He removes an item that I can't make out and puts it in his pocket. He walks out of the room and disappears. Now in front of me is a hallway where the ceiling is lined with a grey smoke. For me, the appearance of this grey means sadness, negativity, or something more sinister.

At the end of the hall stands the stern woman from the fireplace, her back to me as she looks out the window. Down this hallway are seven doors, three on one side and four on the other. The first two empty rooms have white walls and are filled with the toys of little girls.

The third room on the left does not have a door. The walls are blue and the room contains one single bed on the right wall and a crib on the left. The names "Mathew" and "Arthur" echo through the room. I go straight to the single bed where a boy of about five years is tucked tightly into the sheets. The sheets seem to be freshly pressed and starched. They are tucked so tightly around the boy - too tightly.

I soon notice this is not a sleeping child. His lips are shades of blue, the color gone from his face. His eyes are open ever so slightly. I am afraid to turn. Afraid to look at the crib.

I take my time, but the crib is empty, all the linens stripped from the mattress.

I cross the hall to a pink room with two identical single beds. They are empty except for the fresh bundle of flowers tied with twine that lay on each made bed. Between the beds is a table with an assortment of medical glass bottles, clothes, and bowls. The only name that echoes is "Lilly".

I exit the room to see that the stern woman is still standing at the window at the end of the hall. I make my way behind her and look over her shoulder. She watches two children aged about four and seven years playing on hay bales. Two teenaged boys nearby watch the children as they play.

It was in this moment I see she holds something: a bundle. All I can think is that they are the sheets that had been stripped from the crib in the blue room.

Suddenly, the silence is broken by voices; I spin, trying to determine their source. Following the sounds, I find the stern woman now in the kitchen with the man. The conversation is tinny, like it is playing through a child's string-and-can telephone. Though their voices are warped, I try to piece their words together.

She paces and yells. The man tells her they need to leave; that they need a fresh start; that they have to follow the money. She says she can't leave because this is the last place her babies knew. He says they can rent the house out and come back one day. He insists that they need to go south because the sickness hasn't reached there yet.

I see the understanding dawning on her face, a sort of resignation that settles as the sternness melts away. They had built this place for their family. Together she and her love had put everything they had into this house. She only ever wanted family there, but now there is nothing left of that dream.

At this moment, I feel I understand what happened her. I begin to feel that I am intruding. I know I've gotten answers, in one of the clearest experiences I had ever had. I cross the floors to the front living room, back to where I started, sit on that same couch, close my eyes, and start my process of coming back to my own reality.

When I first received that call from Frank, I used my intuition to try decipher what this could be. A demon? Poltergeist? Ghost? Going into the house I knew nothing of the history, nothing of the people who lived there. I only knew what he had told me.

After coming back to my reality, I just sat in awe. In my whole life I had never had such a clear experience. Usually I would get one thought, maybe a few names or one scene, but this played out like a movie. I felt like *I* was haunting *them*.

I looked to Susan, the stack of my index cards looking heavy in her hands. Frank's face had turned a particular shade of white, and I asked if I had scared them. He replied that he was simply shocked because he had never seen anything like that before.

Frank excused himself as Susan and I went to the table and spread out the assortment of notecards. I was taken aback by the amount of information she had been able to collect from my rambling.

"I didn't expect that," Susan said the corners of her mouth pulling down, still in some sort of shock-induced trance. "I always believed in that stuff but … You knew about the cemetery, you got the names… So many of the names."

Frank came back into the room and placed a picture on the table in front of me. Staring up at me from the photo was the stern lady with the large mole and the even larger scar, her hair pulled tight into a bun. He explained that this was a picture he had found under the buffet I had mentioned; it was his grandmother, who left the house in 1934. He then proceeded to tell me the history of the house and his family.

Frank's relatives had built the sprawling house decades earlier, but in 1934, the family boarded the windows, took only what they could carry, and moved to southern Ontario. Their plan had been to use the large eight-bedroom house as a summer home, but due to

circumstances, that never came to be. The
family never visited the home again. Luckily,
the family had some wealth and paid a local
man to maintain the property and keep up with
the home so it never fell into disrepair.

When Frank's estranged mother
inherited the house in 1967, she never told a
soul. There was a trust left by her father to be
used only for the home's maintenance. Frank
only found out about the house, its history, and
his inheritance from a lawyer in the weeks after
his mother passed.

In March 2013, overwhelmed by
excitement, Frank and Susan loaded up their
minivan and set out on a two-hour adventure to
find the secret house. When they had arrived
they found that the groundskeeper Harold had
left them a letter, which read like so.

Frank and Susan:

I hope you enjoy your new home. I have included a set of keys in the mail box. All that was ever done to the inside was repair work, your usual dusting and cleaning. All linens were stripped from the beds in rooms 2-4-6 last year and burned due to mould. Luckily there is no mould anywhere else in the house. Your mother had the electrical redone in 2009 and a new furnace/ac installed in 2010. This house really is a treasure and a real time capsule. It has always weighed heavily on my family that such a beautiful place was not lived in. We hope you can bring life back into it. We think it would make the spirits less restless.

Harold.

Ps- please leave a letter in the front mailbox of what you would like done and your future plans for the home. We will be back Wednesday.

     Frank and Susan unlocked the front door and entered the home that had been unlived-in for so long. They walked quietly through the house as if they were afraid to disturb the family that had been gone for nearly 100 years. Harold was right: the house was a time capsule. The amount of time putting together a home this stunning would have taken forever, and a lot of money back in the era that it was built.

The outside looked like a basic red brick farmhouse, but the inside was stunning. The walls were lined with dark cherry wood, the ceilings all had crown mouldings and plaster art. On from the foyer was a staircase that wrapped around the twenty-five-foot-wide hallway. On the left and right of the hall were oversized openings that entered into two large living rooms. One had lush Victorian carpeting, a stunning master piano and oversized settees. Old art and mirrors covered almost all the walls.

The room to the right held a fifteen-foot dining table with all matching captain's chairs. In the front great room was a large desk and an angry-looking taxidermy black bear; beyond that was another sitting room that featured more oversized, plush Victorian armchairs.

In the back of the house they found a library lined with musty old books and five children's desks. Around the corner was a completely white kitchen with glass-paned cupboards, and off the kitchen was a tall atrium, the glass green from years of sun.

Since the house was so large it felt to them as if it took ten minutes the climb the stairs, which were made of the same dark wood as the foyer. Mirrors of all sizes and shapes lined the walls on the side of the staircase. Every step brought them to a new mirror, their faces either warped from the years of heat and moisture or speckled by aging that lined reflective surface.

Once they reached the landing they separated to explore the rooms. They found eight bedrooms of varying sizes, some set up with a crib or child's bed, or filled with furniture draped with white sheets. Down a separate hall were four identical three-piece bathrooms tiled from floor to ceiling.

Frank and Susan spent two hours in the walls of the home that they now owned, exploring each cranny, each drawer and every corner. They didn't say a word to each other until they were both back out on the front porch. Susan had tears in her eyes and expressed to Frank that she had never seen anything so beautiful. They decided that they had to do something with the place, not sell it like they had first discussed.

The commute was too far from their jobs and it would be too difficult to maintain just as a vacation house. So, after a dinner out and a few glasses of wine, the couple decided to turn the house into a bed and breakfast. The inheritance Frank received from his mother was not a lot, but it was enough to live off of while the couple got the house ready and transitioned to back country living.

Over the next few months, they worked closely with Harold on getting the home into top shape so they could take guests. It wasn't until they started modifying the bedrooms, replacing beds and curtains that the strange things began. They had pulled all of the existing furniture in Rooms 2-4-7 into the middle of each room so that the walls were easy to access for a fresh coat of paint. Susan had just finished her last room when she popped down the hall to use the restroom. She was gone maybe three minutes and left all the doors open so the rooms could have good airflow for the drying paint.

After she finished, Susan was walking down the hall when she noticed that all the doors that she had propped open with rocks were closed. Thinking perhaps Frank was up to something, she called for him, but there was no reply. She opened the door to the room she had most recently painted. All the air was immediately sucked out of her chest.

The furniture that had been in a mass in the middle of the room was all back in its original spots - against the freshly painted wet walls. Susan threw open the doors to the other two rooms. Just like the first room, all the furniture that had been in the middle of the room was back in its original place, against the wet freshly painted walls.

That was when Susan remembered that Frank wasn't even on the property; he had gone into town an hour ago for supplies. She was all alone in that large, desolate house. All she knew was that whatever had moved that much furniture in total silence in a matter of minutes had more power then she could force herself to imagine.

When Frank returned home, Susan showed him what had happened; he tried - but failed – to come up with an explanation. After a long day of silence he went to Susan and promised that if something else big happened, they would contact someone who could help.

That night Frank conducted some web research and found that when someone invades a place that has been so desolate for a long time it can cause some weird disturbances, but that in most cases it wasn't something to be too worried about. In his head he was going to do whatever it took to make this venture work. He had left his job, his friends and life to make this dream come true. There was no way some little ghost or activity from god knows what was going to ruin this for his family.

That night, Susan woke Frank at 2.22 am. He was covered in a cold sweat and she was standing appalled with her hands in tight fists against her chest. Her face was white and tears streamed from her eyes. Frank flew from bed, but Susan cowered, falling to the floor and screaming. She pressed her body as tightly as she could fit into the corner of the west wall. It took her a few moments to realise that her husband was now awake, that the screaming voice that had emanated from his lips was gone. She stuttered, trying to explain to Frank that he had been beating his hands as hard as he could against the bed and screaming in a loud, drunken, thick accent, louder than she thought any man could.

White-faced and stunned, Frank sat back and tried to remember what he had been dreaming about. His dreams that night were not anything like she had explained. In his sleep he had been imagining himself playing with his old dog in the yard of a friend's house. He wondered if perhaps Susan had been having some kind of waking nightmare.

It took an hour for Susan's blood pressure to regulate. For fear that such an event might happen again, Frank slept alone in the last bedroom down the hall.

Things stayed quiet for the remainder of the two months they had set aside to finish the renovations. On June 21st, Susan set up an online contest to attract potential customers to the new bed and breakfast. If you came to the bed and breakfast's Facebook page and then liked and shared it, you would be entered into a drawing for a free night's stay at the inn before they opened. The couple was blown away by the response, and at the end of the week chose five winners: two young adults in their twenties, a single senior man, and an adult mother-daughter duo.

Everyone arrived around five pm and was shown to their respected rooms. Then all enjoyed a catered celebration dinner, after which each guest toured the grounds and the house. The guests were also captivated and taken aback by the beauty and detail that Frank and Susan had also fallen for.

After they had toured the house, the mother and daughter duo opted for a nightcap downstairs with Frank and Susan. They spent hours talking about the town and the home's history. The young couple had taken over one of the upstairs bathrooms.
The older gentleman had kept quiet at dinner and was now wandering the grounds and taking pictures.

Around 10 pm the older man entered the living room where Frank, Susan, and the mother-daughter duo sat talking. Joining the foursome, he asked Susan a strange question: would she mind if he read a story to her son when they put him down to sleep?

Susan stood abruptly, explaining to the man that there were no children on the premises. The man put his hand to his mouth in surprise, he explained that he had just been to the end of the hall that held the guest rooms. As he approached the last room on the left, he saw the door was open. Curious, he peeked inside and discovered a young boy playing on the floor. The youngster was laughing and talking out loud. He looked up to the old man and said his name was Arthur, and that he was six years old.

Frank and Susan dashed for the stairs, pushing quickly past the old man. They knew that the last room on the left was kept locked, as it was reserved for storage, that all the furniture was scattered and covered with sheets.

They took the stairs three at a time before stopping at the entrance to the hallway. As they looked down the hall, they saw that the last door on the left was indeed open. Frank led the way with Susan right on his heels. Before she could see inside the room, she saw the look on Frank's face. He had gone white as a ghost. Susan brushed past him to discover that all the furniture in place, and a pile of folded sheets sat on top of the freshly-made bed – sheets they had thrown out the previous month. In the middle of a room was a large puddle of muddy water.

By this time the mother-daughter duo and the older gentleman were behind them, squeaks and gasps coming from their mouths. It was only a few hours earlier that Frank had opened this room using the large key ring to show them an example of what the house had been like when they first arrived. Everyone there that night knew this room was not in a livable state.

Frank entered the room and reached down to touch the water; it was oily and warm. No words were exchanged until the older man spoke up. He said that he had seen things like this before, and now he would conclude his stay. He thanked Susan and Frank for their hospitality and was gone within the hour.

The mother-daughter duo was more intrigued then anything, though Frank and Susan felt hesitant to discuss what had just happened. They didn't want to be known as a haunted attraction, and in this moment they didn't know how to react.

They asked the duo to please not tell the young couple. They pointed out their bedroom in case the women needed anything, then said their goodnights. They spent the rest of the evening talking the event over, trying to figure out what exactly had happened. Was it a paranormal occurrence? Was it some sort of prank? Had they left the door unlocked?

At one am, Frank was ripped out of sleep by a loud noise followed by booming sounds against the wall. He leapt out of bed to investigate, while Susan stayed where she was. It quickly became obvious that the sounds were coming from the room that the young twenty-something couple was residing in.

Screaming for the couple, Frank pulled on the door and tried to pry it open, but it wouldn't budge. He heard the sounds of shuffling and furniture sliding.

The door finally burst open; the couple flew out of the room and slammed into the opposite wall with such force that they left holes in the plaster. Breathing heavily, the man stared back into the room, his eyes dark puddles of fear, his mouth open as if he couldn't get enough air. His girlfriend was already down the hall holding onto the banister and crying like a scared child. Frank stood shaking in the doorway. He tried flipping the light switch - nothing.

The couple finally found their voices. The young lady said she was awoken by a pull on her hair. Thinking it was her boyfriend, she went to push him, only to find he was facing the opposite way. She then reached for the bedside lamp, but it wouldn't turn on.

Feeling the first tickle of panic, she shook her boyfriend awake. Once roused, he also found the light on his table did not work. He sat up and searched the top of the table for his cellphone, but felt nothing. In that moment, he knew something was really wrong.

It wasn't as if the room was just "dark" - it was beyond dark. The whole room was absent of any light. Along with this blacker-than-black room was a complete absence of sound. Beginning to panic, the couple sprang from the bed and started feeling their way around the room. The pressure of the silence was building fast in their ears, a pressure that was becoming painful in the way your ears hurt when you dive too deep in a pool.

The furniture was not as it had been when they'd gone to sleep. Their panic and anxiety quickened when the couple realized they couldn't find the door. At that moment, the couple claimed that out of the deafening silence, they heard a woman's voice say right in their ears, "You were not invited."

Adrenalin took over and the man started ripping the furniture from the walls, trying to find a way out. Finally, he heard Frank banging on the other side of one wall and discovered a heavy oak armoire was pushed up against the door. The couple were able to pull the armoire away and finally escape the room.

It wasn't until after Frank and Susan had the couple wrapped in blankets on the front porch with a cup of tea that they took a flash light into the room to investigate. Susan walked carefully to each of the three lamps and tried to turn the little black switches so she could fill the room with light. Not only would the lights not turn on, she discovered that they light bulbs were gone. Not broken - gone.

The couple refused to go back into the house to collect their belongings. Frank packed for them and apologized. The couple barely mumbled a response; the shock of the situation had stolen all their words.

The mother and daughter duo were fast on their tails - the whole night was just too much for them to handle. They explained that after being woken by the banging and screams, they were accompanied down the stairs by a reflection of a little girl in the mirrors that framed the entire stairway wall.

After their guests departed, Frank spent the rest of the night looking for some kind of help. That was when he found me.

Together, we reviewed everything and came to a conclusion. Since the house was left sitting for so long, the presence of living humans was a big wakeup to whatever energy was still there. Frank's grandmother's want for only family to be there had been so strong that it was affecting them nearly one hundred years later.

Frank and Susan seemed shocked by the things I saw, and what they heard me say. To be honest, I was shocked too. The hole behind the picture in the bedroom over the bed was quite the find for them. It was full of many documents.

They got out the family bible and read to me the names I had mentioned, along with their deaths and the reasons they happened. It didn't end there. Frank brought out another picture of his grandmother, the woman who I had described by mentioning the large birthmark and scar that was also evident in the photograph. We then walked out to the hidden cemetery I had seen while in "that reality". The names of the children matched the aged, hard-to-read stones that stood in a line.

The local paranormal group arrived that afternoon. With them was a medium who tried to connect to the spirits and help them understand. I left right after they arrived as the reading had taken way more out of me then I assumed it would, and I needed to sleep. In my absence, the team conducted a full investigation and came up with a couple low-level EVPs and one questionable photo.

Having done all I could, I returned home. I received a call from Frank and Susan two months after my visit. They told me that they made one more attempt at using the home as a bed and breakfast. Unfortunately, the same kind of events unfolded. They wanted my opinion on what I personally thought they should do. I am not an opinionated person; I tend to keep what I think is "right" to myself. However, I told them that I thought if they just used the house as their own, there would be no further issues.

Frank's grandmother's desperate energy after losing those babies had left too large of an impression on the house, and perhaps she would only welcome family members into her home.

A month after that I received a final call. Frank and Susan let me know that they had sat at the kitchen table and explained to the open air that they were family, and from now on, they would be the only ones who would reside on the estate. From that night forward the house was in perfect peace.

THE DARKNESS

I met Pastor John in the fall of 2011. He contacted me after reaching out to a parapsychology firm based out of Niagara Falls, New York. Three weeks before his phone call, two sisters in search of answers had approached him. Now they required my help.

Kerry was the older sister at the young age of 21. She was petite and stood at 5 foot. She had a quiet, kind demeanor, blonde hair, and blue eyes. She was someone you would find very approachable. Her 20-year-old sister Christina was taller and darker in every way. Her hair was dark brown and hung halfway down her back, and her eyes were the brightest green I have ever seen.

These two women were both in their second year at the University of Toronto. Originally from North Bay, Ontario, they had moved in with their grandmother to attend university. Their grandmother was an exuberant, joyful lady, who became even more ecstatic when she found her precious granddaughters had been accepted to U of T. She quickly suggested that they live with her while they did their schooling. The first year went flawlessly; the grandmother packed the girls' lunches and the girls helped with the upkeep around the house.

Sadly, during the summer between their first year and second, Kerry and Christina woke up in the middle of the night to find their grandmother dead on the couch, her knitting needles still in her hands.

To the girls' surprise, everything was left to them in the will. Their grandmother had always wanted her granddaughters to have the best of everything. The home was located in a prime area of Toronto and was worth more then the girls could have imagined. While the house was very dated and needed a lot of work, the large square almost looked like something that would fit better into England, not Toronto. Their parents thought the best thing to do was to sell the oversized house and get an apartment. All the money from the house would easily pay for all their schooling, cars and then some.

However, the girls were opposed to selling. They knew how much their grandma loved the home and the circular garden she had put so much love into and took such precious care of. Twenty years ago it had started as a mere 5-foot expanse, but now the entire rounded lawn was lush with flowers and plants of every colorful species you could imagine. A 10-foot fence with a locked gate surrounded it to keep out animals, and a 2-foot brick path led up the center to a small circle where a lawn chair and table sat.

Overlooking the garden was the kitchen. Adjacent was a bright green living room complete with a glass table, unicorn knick-knacks, and tacky fabric-bound chairs. Beyond the living room was a small den, a bathroom, and an oversized sitting room that looked onto the gate and busy street. Upstairs, all four bedrooms and the bathroom were clad in floral wallpaper. The girls might not have been fans of the décor, but to them, it was home. They say to this day that they have never felt as home as they did within those walls.

Kerry took her grandmother's death a lot harder than Christina, who already had an understanding of death. At a young age she had lost a best friend in a motor vehicle accident, while Kerry had never lost anyone. When their 94-year-old grandmother had passed, Christina was sad despite having known it was going to happen at some point. She might had been the younger sister, but it hadn't come as a complete shock.

Still, both Kerry and Christina drowned their sadness with partying. Almost every night, the house was full of drunk college students. Each girl began experimenting with drugs almost every night.

As time went on, Christina grew tired of the partying. She knew how disappointed her grandmother would be if she were still alive. In addition, the house was really starting to reflect the state of the girls' minds. The carpets were dirty; the garden had over grown into disarray.

One afternoon after all the prior evening's guests had peeled themselves off the floor, she went to her sister's room. She found

Kerry asleep, completely covered by blankets. Kerry had always been one to sleep on top the blankets as anything made her uncomfortably hot, even clothing. She usually just walked the halls of the house naked.

Christina pulled down the blanket to find her sister naked, her eyes wide open, and a bubbly rash all over her neck, arms, and inner thighs. Christina screamed, but it wasn't until she shook her sister violently that life came back into Kerry's eyes. Christina started crying. She explained to her sister that she needed to smarten up and live. Things were getting too risky, too fast.

Kerry sat up and agreed that she too had grown tired of the endless nights with boys who had a bottomless supply of pills and alcohol. They knew that they were good girls that came from good people. Together, they wanted their lives to reflect the hard work they had put in up to this point.

The rash that covered Kerry's extremities grew larger as the day progressed, and she couldn't stop scratching. Worried, Christina insisted they go to the emergency room. Sitting in the triage chair in front of the nurse, Kerry pulled up her sleeve and showed her arm. The skin was free, clear and unblemished. Christina grabbed Kerry's other arm and pushed the sleeve as high as it would go. Nothing. The girls apologized and and left the hospital shaking their heads. Kerry was just thankful the rash was gone and put it down to stress.

The next day the girls spent every hour of sunlight taming the garden and cleaning the house until it looked as if their grandma was still there. Collapsing on the couch at the end of the day, the girls could barely remember the last few months of their hard lifestyle. It was as if tidying the house had wiped the slate clean. They felt like the two shy, soft-spoken women they had been when they first arrived nearly two years ago.

Later, Kerry agreed to take the last bag of garbage into the kitchen if Christina promised to get a movie started. When the last of the title sequence had played and Kerry still hadn't returned, Christina grew worried and called out for her. There was no response.

Christina made her way to the kitchen and poked her head around the corner. She saw Kerry standing in the middle of the kitchen looking out the window into the darkness outside - the window that overlooked their grandmother's precious garden.

The garbage bag was still in her hand. Christina called for her sister. No response. That was when she noticed the Kerry was whispering a slew of words that were barely loud enough to be heard.

Christina rushed over into her eye line and again called Kerry's name again. Kerry didn't break her gaze or her whispering, but Christina leaned in, and strained her ears to hear what her sister was saying. The words coming from her mouth weren't English, but they weren't pure nonsense, either. They sounded like some kind of primal language. Whatever it was, Christina had never heard it before.

She reached out and grabbed her sister's wrist firmly, trying to break the trance she was in. The second Christina touched Kerry, the girl snapped right out of the episode with an angry look on her face. Kerry quickly asked if the movie was on yet then walked over to the door which was next to the window and dropped the bag outside.

Christina quickly explained everything she just witnessed, how Kerry had been standing like a zombie, looking out the window and speaking in tongues. Kerry's only response was that her sister was lying, and she shouldn't make jokes like that. Christina decided to just forget about the incident, but promised herself to call their mother if anything else strange happened.

The next morning Christina performed her usual Sunday routine of showering, waking her sister up, and then heading downstairs to make coffee. She glanced up to see the sun coming through the window and then screamed, dropping the hot cup full of coffee into the sink with a crash.

The backyard garden was completely destroyed. Every plant and bush had been ripped from the earth and thrown about as if a tornado had passed through the backyard.

Within seconds, Kerry was by her side, speechless. Wordlessly, the girls dashed outside. The gate was still locked, so if someone had entered in the night, they would have had to somehow scale the fence. Christina stepped on something and felt a crunch, and then another.

Lifting the plants, she found two crushed birds. She called for Kerry to grab her a garbage bag. The more flora she picked up, the more birds she found. She wasn't sure what upset her more: the fact that her grandmother's beloved garden her grandma had been destroyed, or that perhaps her sister was losing her mind. Maybe Kerry had something to do with this. Maybe she was the one to blame.

However, all she wanted right now was to clean this all up and forget, but she kept finding more birds. They didn't look as if they'd met a brutal end, more like they were simply sleeping. Once they'd finished, they had 13 dead birds and 7 garbage bags of wilted plants. Kerry suggested making a police report, but Christina knew in a city like Toronto, a possibly vandalized garden wouldn't be too high on their list of priorities.

Later that evening, Christina finally placed a call to her mother. She told her about the rash, Kerry acting strange, and about the events that had unfolded with the garden. Her mother assured her that the girls were under a lot of stress, but she would talk to Kerry. As to the garden, their mother attributed it to some neighbourhood kids who probably trampled the sleeping birds on their way out.

This didn't provide Christina with any comfort. Since the day she found Kerry with the disappearing rash, she knew there was more going on than meets the eye. She had never been a fan of the paranormal, but she had seen enough scary movies to notice how her life was starting to resemble one.

After Kerry spent an hour on the phone with her mother, the girls settled on the couch with some Doritos and the Sunday night cartoon line-up. They flicked off all of the lights except for the shimmering chandelier in the kitchen. Halfway through the evening, the kitchen went black, and they were plunged into darkness, their only light emanating from the television.

Startled, Kerry quickly paused the DVR and both girls stared into the dark room. Suddenly, the sound of a million plates breaking erupted from the kitchen. Both girls sprang to their feet; Christina screamed while Kerry pulled at her cheeks in horror. Abruptly, the light switched back on and the sound halted.

Entering the kitchen, the girls found every cabinet open and every dish smashed on the floor. Even their dining room table was flipped up side down. The girls fled. They went to a motel a few blocks away and called their parents.

Their mother answered with an angry tone. It was obvious they had enough problems at home. She had racked up a pretty hefty debt from gambling over the last few years, and when her own mother died, she saw her opportunity to sell the house and pay off the debt. To say she had been disappointed when she found out her daughters received the inheritance was an understatement. Since losing everything to the girls, she had been less than loving towards them.

Christina explained what happened, but her mother only laughed and assured her there had to be some kind of logical explanation. She told Christina to go online and see if there had been a small earthquake, then said she would be there the next day to investigate the claims. Christina hung up the phone knowing her mother couldn't – or wouldn't - be able to do anything. She needed to take things into her own hands.

Their mom made the trip from North Bay and met the girls at the house at 11 am. She sloshed through the glass in the kitchen in her 4 inch heels and looked at the girls. "Are you sure you didn't just have a party and want me to pay for new dishes because some asshole got rowdy?" she accused. Christina could barely believe what just came out of her mother's mouth.

Her mother continued to laugh, but this time with some hesitation. "If you didn't do this then I suggest you get a priest. Did you play with a Ouija board or something?" The nerves were gone and it was apparent she found her joke to be far wittier than it actually was. "I don't know what to tell you," she continued. "As long as you haven't been hurt I wouldn't put to much thought into it. Sometimes you need to just ignore this type of stuff and it will go away."

With that, their mother was back on the road and the girls were in the kitchen filling old boxes with mountains of glass. Christina and Kerry were both appalled that their mother didn't have more to say about the situation, and were overcome with anger that she simply did not care. Kerry and Christina shared a look of disappointment. How could something as petty as inheritance warrant such apathy?

That Tuesday, Christina found her way to the pastor's office. She marched in with determination, and before even saying hello she was showing him pictures on her phone of the plants, birds, Kerry's rash, and the kitchen.

The pastor himself had a 34-year-old daughter and felt much sympathy for the girls. He promised to be by that evening to bless the house, though he wasn't sure what he believed. During his decades at the church he had seen many strange and miraculous things, but he also knew that sometimes a simple blessing could settle whatever energy lingered.

The evening approached much faster then the pastor expected. It was 8 pm when he made his way up the five cement stairs to the address Christina had left him. As he reached for the bell, Christina opened the door with

Kerry cowering behind her. She thanked him for coming and both girls moved out of the doorway. The pastor felt the fear as it emanated off the girls. He questioned himself for a moment on what he might be getting into.

At first glance, the home seemed clean, well kept, and large. He explained that he would go from room to room and bless each area individually. Instead of starting with the main floor he headed to the stairs, working from top to bottom. He moved from the bathroom to Christina's room and then the spare room to Kerry's room. He took note that as he entered Kerry's room it was at least ten degrees warmer than the other rooms he'd just been in. The room looked clean and tidy in every way, but it had a slight undertone of a rancid garbage smell.

The pastor opened his book and raised the cross in his right hand. As soon as he did, the cross flew from his hand. It went soaring right under the bed and his hand snapped back into his body like a sand bag. He didn't say a word. He left the cross and walked down the narrow hall to the top of the stairs. He found Kerry directly at the bottom looking up at him. He described what had just unfolded as the redness went from his cheeks to his neck.

He reached the bottom of the steps, but Kerry didn't move. He realized that she was still looking at the top of the stairs and that she had never been looking directly at him at all.

Christina rounded the corner and surveyed the situation. She reached out and took her sister's hand, and Kerry instantly burst back into reality. She gasped for air as if she had just been fetched from a near drowning and collapsed onto her knees. The pastor reached down and helped her stand, and anxiously asked if she was okay. Kerry replied that she had just "sneezed". At this moment Christina and the pastor's eyes met with understanding.

The pastor asked the girls to meet him in the living room. They all took opposite seats from each other at the glass table. Kerry finally settled back into a regular breathing pattern. The pastor started explaining that not all scary stories we hear are just make believe. Sometimes in rare situations there was something beyond our control that could invade the lives of regular people. Kerry just stared at the table while Christina asked in a small, broken voice what they could do next.

The pastor told her that he had enough reason to believe that what the girls were experiencing would only evolve and get worse. He promised to devise a plan and call the girls within the next few days. He left them with a bible, his phone number, and a crucifix.

When he got up to leave, Kerry was still sitting in her daze, so Christina rose to walk him out. When Christina and the pastor reached the front porch, he took the opportunity to explain that he thought whatever was going on in the home seem directly linked to Kerry. Christina shook her head. Though she'd suspected for some time that her sister was somehow the cause of the events, a pang of denial resonated within her.

    The next day the pastor used his connections to find someone who could help, and he called me. He didn't want a psychic. He needed two very different and specific types of people. Besides me, he called upon a man from upstate New York who had an extensive education when it came to parapsychology and demonology.

    When I first received the pastor's call I was impressed that he had already been briefed to not give me any details. I ask not to be told details as I never want my subconscious to have any ideas when I enter a case. He only explained to me that this case entailed two young women, one single detached home, and I would be working with another person from the paranormal field. He asked how soon I could come. I assured him I could be there the day after next.

When I reached the house, the pastor greeted me at the front gate. He shook my hand and thanked me for coming on such short notice, then commented how surprised he was that I was so young. We turned to the house when I felt his hand on my shoulder. I turned back to the pastor to see him frowning.
"Put on a good front when you go in there," he warned. At that moment, I felt nervous. I usually get some kind of "feeling" before I walk into a place, but this house felt like any normal family home.

I met Christina, shook her hand, and thanked her for inviting me into her home. With my index cards in hand,I made my way to the family room where I saw a couple of arm chairs, a couch, and a large flat screen TV. I took a seat on the couch, focusing my eyes on the clock that hung on the yellow wall above the doorway.

As my eyes adjust, I feel the familiar sensation of pins and needles that so often accompany me when I make connections. I feel a mature, female energy, and see an outline of a short, squat woman. She emanates only a pure loving energy.
Next is the kitchen. Here, I pick up a strong smell of ozone, and panic settles in my chest. As I walk, I hear the sound of someone shuffling through glass, but I see nothing when I look down. The light in the kitchen dissolves into night and I hear the muffled sound of a yell. I turn back towards the family room.
The room that was just free and clear now fills with a frightening negative energy. Dark grey and black fog curls its way along the roof

from the family room. I squint my eyes as the grey takes over my vision. I am blinded by the dark fog and can't see the family room at all. I feel along the walls until I find the door. Coughing, I turn back to look at the room.

I see where the darkness is pouring from. Over by one armchair is a dark black mass, and all around it the blackness erupts and oozes like an obsidian waterfall.

A buzzing overtakes my senses. My breathing tightens, and suddenly my ears are full of the sound of 1000 swarming blackflies. I press the palms of my hands into my eyes as hard as I can, trying to snap out of it. I sense that I can lift my head, and I slowly pull my hands away from my face. The sweat drips from my forehead onto my cheeks.

My vision suddenly faded and instead of empty space where the darkness had come from, a tiny young blonde woman stood. The occupancy of the room had grown to 5 people: Christina, the pastor, the blonde girl, and a dark Romanian-looking man. No one said anything, just stared at me.

"Who are you?" I asked the blonde girl in what I hoped was a friendly tone. She introduced herself as Kerry, Christina's sister who also lived in the home. I walked to her, feeling razor-bladed butterflies in my stomach. I reached out to shake her hand. As soon as we were about to connect, a loud bang rang out from upstairs. I looked quickly to the pastor, who nodded as if he knew what I was about to do. I grabbed Kerry's hand, and instantly my vision was gone again.

Black. Instead of getting a sense of how she was feeling or who she was, I only felt a rendering of a soul. I had only encountered this once before. This was a woman who had already been through the manifestation, infestation and oppression stages of demonic possession. I can only have my abilities completely shut down when reading a person if the energy had been corrupted by something truly dark. Letting go of Kerry, I walked around Christina to see if I sensed the same about her. There was anxiety, but no darkness like in Kerry's grip.

I approached the pastor and the Romanian man who introduced himself as a colleague. I asked if I could speak to them both outside. After we left the house, I explained my findings, and both men nodded their heads. They agreed with my observations. The Romanian's name was Costel, and he was a well-respected demonologist. Although he was not approved to do exorcisms, he was highly trained and had assisted in nearly 45 cases. They told me that they needed three people to confirm their theory to move forward.

Within a moment, we were back in the family room sitting with the girls. As the pastor asked the girls why they thought this might have started, I kept my eyes trained on Kerry.

Christina explained how their grandmother had passed and how they had been using drugs and drinking excessively. (Don't get me wrong, drugs and alcohol are not always a gate way to the paranormal, but when you use it for certain reasons it can open an unwanted can of worms.) Kerry started breathing heavily as if she was having a panic attack, she then got up and tried to catch her breath. She suddenly collapsed to the floor, and we all ran to her in panic. As Christina rolled her onto her back, Kerry started laughing hysterically in a low tone that didn't match her sweet face.

Costel picked her up, and with the help of the pastor, they carried her to the spare bedroom upstairs. Christina hadn't gotten off the floor. I knelt beside her and moved her hair, inching closer to comfort her. "I didn't think things like this could happen," she whispered as I held her in my arms. "I don't want to lose her."

I asked her if there was anything Kerry hadn't told us. I knew that falling into a depression and leaning on substance abuse was enough to draw in that kind of negative energy, but I also knew that this energy had moved extremely quickly. Christina walked to the window. "I promised her I would never tell." She mumbled. I explained that what she wasn't telling me might be what saved her.

Then came the truth. She sat in the closest red arm chair and laid out the facts. A month after their grandmother passed they met a two drifters at a local bar the university kids hung out at. They were handsome and had alluring, mysterious foreign accents. The boys had paid attention to the two girls all night and kept the drinks coming. Kerry had suggested after last call was announced that they should all head back to the house for more drinks. Kerry had always loved mysterious men, but Christina was always drawn to the football type. Nonetheless, Christina agreed. Once 4 am rolled around she could barely keep her eyes open, and when Kerry told her they were going to watch a movie, she opted for bed.

The next morning, Christina found Kerry laying on the kitchen floor in only a bra. Green welts covered her legs and arms. Christina rushed to her side to find Kerry awake, staring up at the ceiling. Christina frantically rushed for the phone to call for help. Behind her, Kerry stood up, swaying a bit as she reached for the phone before smashing it into the wall. Kerry claimed that she and the boys hooked up, and even though it got a little rough, everything was fine.

Christina knew better, as Kerry was actually quite the prude. Her sister went off to shower; afterward, she acted as if nothing happened. Every time Christina brought it up, Kerry snapped at her and threatened to leave. She started to use drugs excessively and get blackout drunk. It wasn't long after that when everything started to happen.

I knew that those men had invaded her body and soul. That was enough to tear someone apart and reach a devastating level of despair. I thanked Christina and assured her Kerry would not find out she'd shared this sensitive information. I passed on what I had learned to the pastor and Costel.

The four of us sat around Christina as Costel explained to Kerry what was going to take place that evening. If they didn't take action tonight, things would get a lot worse. Kerry began to cry.

I had never seen an exorcism conducted before, but it definitely didn't follow the exact script of those you see in the movies. Costel placed two armchairs across from one another in the spare bedroom. Kerry sat in one with only her ankles tied to the feet of the chair. Her crying hadn't stopped since we'd told her our plan. In front of her sat Costel, and to her left stood the pastor. I was on her right with Christina, who stood behind her bracing on Kerry's shoulders.

Costel turned out the light. He lit nine candles and some incense and played a track from a burned disk he had brought. Calming nature sounds filled the room. Kerry's face kept changing expression and colors as we moved forward. Our chants intensified, repeating what Costel asked us. Her crying became louder and hysterical.

Ten minutes into the chants, Kerry became silent. "I can feel it," she gasped. Her small blue fingers circled tightly around the arms of the chair. A bubbling sound erupted from her mouth followed by a maniacal giggle.

The laughter sounded of three separate voices: a man, a child, and an elderly woman.

As Christina lifted her hands from Kerry's shoulders, Costel yelled to her not to break the bond. I grabbed her arm and pulled her close again. After an hour, Costel stretched his neck. Christina then randomly started to press down hard on her sister's shoulders and started yelling.

Yelling that she needed her.

Yelling that she wasn't going to let her go.

Yelling that she was sorry.

Yelling that whatever was inside her sister was not going to win.

Costel and the pastor started praying. The room got hot, then nauseatingly cold. Kerry went limp.

Costel checked Kerry's pulse. It was regular. The blue tint to her skin was dissipating, and somehow her feet were untied.

Costel carried her to her room and laid her on the bed. He hooked up the heart monitor he had brought, then walked to the three of us waiting in the hall and shut the door behind him.

We sat up the remainder of the night. We talked preventative measures and traded stories.

At 6.30 am we heard a shower turn on upstairs and Christina burst into tears at the sound. She shared that her sister hadn't showered in nearly a week. We told her that that could have been be another sign of demonic invasion.

At 7 am, Kerry stepped into the kitchen. I had not met this person before. Her skin was alive and her eyes had a sparkle. She stood in the doorway with no words in her mouth. I walked to her, and instead of taking her hand, I hugged her.

I didn't feel any darkness at all.

She gingerly sat down at the table. Holding her sister's hand, she thanked us all. Gratitude emanated from her smile.

It has been 5 years since that night. The pastor retired, perhaps not long after this event. Costel now works in the church. Kerry is married with a beautiful daughter of her own, and Christina followed her best friend and fiancé to Texas. The darkness we conquered never returned.

THE DREAMS

It was 2009, a year marred by the aftermath of the financial crisis of '08. In this time, I was still very quiet about the paranormal side of my life. Like many fresh high school grads, I was thrown into the turbulent waters of an uncertain future. I slid through all kinds of niches, trying to find a persona and profession that would help me fit into the world.

I knew I didn't want to be a waitress anymore, nor did I want to rot my life away in retail like so many of my peers. I was trapped floating between disciplines, always starting but never definitively finishing anything. I completed a single semester of police foundations to find running, fighting, and social security was definitely not my forte.

After a flurry of experimentation, I settled on a single pursuit: photography. As a young child, I had an obsession with cameras and almost always had one glued to my body. As a teen, my then "new boyfriend" surprised me with a beautiful Canon camera. I was so fascinated with all the different lenses and attachments that could make each image so unique. Now as an adult, I returned to the same fascination with creating images.

I took to Facebook and created a contest for a free photo shoot. I had so many entries, yet I was drawn to a particular local musician. We'd gone to the same high school, but were in very different circles. I saw her face maybe twice during my high school career.

The musician was insanely talented. Her voice was a rich mixture of country and eclectic indie longing. She told me that she was making her first EP and needed album art. We spent the entire day making our way around the city gathering ideas from taking pictures in over grown corn fields to sultry pictures in the middle of a gravel road in the back country that barely anyone ever used.

A few nights after our photo shoot, I had a dreamed that involved the spirit of a young man. He sat smiling on a broken tree in the middle of a hazy field. He seemed to be a teenager, around 16. The scene was bathed in light and flowers flourished all around him. The tall, handsome boy just sat and looked at me. Words flowed from his coy smile as he spoke to someone out of my field of knowledge.
"You, in that yellow dress..." he grinned.
 "I love those chubby cheeks," he blushed.
"I know about the parties!" he teased.
And then he said something slightly darker, slightly more somber.

"It didn't hurt; I didn't even know till it was over."

He shared with me other comments, some of advice and some of opinion, which are best only repeated to the one they were meant for.

The next night the dream returned. This time the the land was more barren. Its lush greens and emeralds swung into sepia. Tonight he didn't utter a word; instead, he spent the entire night sitting on a log and just looking into my eyes.

As I woke up the next morning I knew that this had to be more then a dream. How could I see him twice in a row? How could it feel so real? I sat perplexed, my eyes felt tired as if they had spent the entire night trained on his.

That night, I was ready. I put a notebook beside my bed with a pen, ready to jot down anything he said.

My comforter was soft; a cool breeze blew in through the window and quickly took me into a dream state. That night I was only with him for a minute. The night was dark and heavy. Suffocating in the darkness of the the dream, I was restless. I jolted awake at 2am, 4am and 5am.

Finally, as the sun broke through the trees outside of my bedroom, I fell asleep, but whatever mysterious dreams had plagued me weren't done yet. I was rocked into an expanse of cold, arid land scorned by the distinct burn of a winter drought. The teen boy appeared once more and walked towards me. He looked right through me and into my soul. I was shaken by the furious heat of his gaze.

"You need to tell her." His hands grasped each other then he pressed them against his chest.

This same dream followed every night for two weeks. I began to dread going to bed. I knew I would spend my entire evening standing in front of him while he repeated his plea that I "tell her". I asked whom I should tell, but I never got an answer. I felt entrapped by the desperado.

By the second week I spent my evenings on the computer through 2am, staring blankly at the sheet of paper I had covered with the scribbles of what the boy had told me. I knew I wasn't even going to sleep. I felt so guilty that I couldn't help him. I had never had a spirit come to me in dream form, and it seemed that to sleep was to be stuck in a dream world where I was nothing but a spectator to the angst around me.

I went on Facebook to distract my over-tired mind. Scrolling through my news feed, I saw the name of the musician I'd photographed. I decided I would do some late night lurking and clicked on her profile picture looking to see if she had used any of the photos we took.

Half an hour later I was still scrolling through years and years of her photos when one practically jumped off the screen.

It was the boy from my dreams.

Beside him was the musician in a yellow formal dress.

My heart pounded. Searching the screen for a possible mistake. I scrolled down hoping to find a comment from him, but no. All I found was comments saying how everyone missed him. I felt a lump form in my throat.

I thought now I might be able to sleep in peace. I was wrong. As soon as my head hit the pillow, I awoke in the field. There was a single tree standing in front of a house. The boy walked to me.

"Now that you know, you have to tell her the things I told you. She needs to hear them." He put his hand on my shoulder. It was the strangest moment as I could actually feel the touch. Just like that I was brought out of my dream. That was the last night I ever dreamed of the boy.

I wrote to the girl on Facebook and let her know I needed to talk with her as soon as possible. I made the call an hour later. As soon as she answered the phone I could already hear the tears in her throat. She knew exactly what this was.

I told her of the boy in the field, of the bits and pieces he told me. I slowly explained I had a connection to the paranormal. I could feel her emotion pulsing through the palpitations of her breath on the phone. I took my time relaying to her the information he shared with me over the past couple weeks. Some was good, serving her the guidance she needed from him, some was just memories and telling her the things he wanted her to know the most.

That day I learned that he was her boyfriend. They had always been together, and were truly in love. The morning he passed he was on his way to see her. His life ended as his car careened into a tree off the road in a field.

It was the most emotional phone call I have ever placed. Both of us cried on either end of the line. I felt honored that I could bring her the peace that she had been looking for all these years. That this was the sign she had been asking for.

The following dream occurred in October 2011.

Two heavy red velvet curtains pull slowly to their respective sides to reveal a beautiful blonde haired, blue-eyed woman. She is standing along a tree line. The smile on her face is full, gleaming with good news. Her ruby lips open to spit out some pretty strange words. "My name is Bobo and I'm dead in the forest". The happiness evaporates. She walks directly back into the tree line.

To say that I spent the next day perplexed is an understatement. Bobo? Bobo? What kind of name was that? I became frustrated that I didn't have much to work with, and so I typed "Bobo" into Google to see what I could find.

I was taken aback: in April of 2011, twenty-year-old American Holly Bobo vanished. The last sighting of her was by her brother. He had seen her walking with a man in camouflage along the forest near their family home. This was all the information I could find on the internet at the time. I kept the story close to my heart knowing a strange girl calling from Canada wasn't going to be any help, especially a strange girl having dreams.

It wasn't until 2014 that there was a break in the case. I had gone on Google every few months to check if there were any developments. The day I did my next search was the day her remains were found.

Holly Bobo's remains were found in the forest right beside her family home.
It was a shock, but being a logical person I tried to chalk it up to coincidence. I didn't have cable so maybe I had subconsciously seen her name on a paper somewhere? I'm not sure but that is a story I will never forget.

In December of 2008, I found myself single again. I was in grade 12 and had always shaped myself around the people I dated. Being single made me feel uncomfortable. Dating apps were new things at the time and I found myself joining a dating site called Zoosk. On this app you met people determined by distance.

This is where 17-year-old me met 28-year-old Michael Rafferty. He had told me he was staying at a friend's while his house was being built, and he taught salsa dance to the seniors at the 50+ center. He sounded like an all-around nice guy.

As I said, I was only 17 years old. I had never met anyone from the internet and found the whole idea quite terrifying, and Michael had gotten - for lack of a better word - "creepy" rather quickly. I liked the attention he was giving me, but I told him I wasn't very interested and wouldn't be giving him my cell phone number.

In the early hours of the morning I was startled by a harsh knocking on my bedroom door. When I opened the door my brother came straight to my window and pointed.

At the end of our driveway was a Honda Civic. Neither of us had any idea who it could be. My dad was already at work and my mother was asleep. I went downstairs and I opened the door, but the car was already down the street.

Later that day, after returning from my lunch break at the office supply store where I worked, one of my coworkers rushed me. She told me a guy had come in and asked for my phone number. She said that since he was cute, she had given it to him. I was more excited then upset to find out who my mystery boy was.

On Friday night I was up watching old reruns when my cell phone rang at 2.30am. I picked up and was greeted by a deep voice. It was Michael from the dating app, and he was the one who had asked for my number from my co-worker.

Everything got weird really quick. He said he wanted to pick me up right now to go tanning. I found that to be creepy, as I had never told him I went tanning. My only reply was that it was 2.30 am. He then told me that he "knew a place". Trying to put him off, I told him that I don't tan. He proceeded to tell me that he had watched me come out of Tan Factory a few times. With that, I hung up and turned my phone off.

A couple days later I pulled out of my driveway to go to my shift at work when I saw the same Honda Civic from a few days prior. It pulled onto the road and followed me to work, parking in the back of the lot.

The car didn't move until I was done my 5-hour shift. Filled with anxiety, I asked one of my male co-workers to walk me out to my car. Luckily, the car did not follow me home. I had an idea that it was Michael following me, but I knew if I told my parents they would be extremely upset I was talking to older men online.

I called Michael that night. As soon as I dialed he picked up.

"Hello?" Michael said. "Celina, it's so good to hea—"

I cut him off in a sharp tone. "Were you following me?"

Michael exhaled and let out a breathy long laugh. "No babe, I would never do that."

My skin crawled. He was acting like he had forgotten about me. I felt stupid and spent the next couple hours talking to him on the phone about totally normal stuff.

We texted for a few weeks, but when he again turned the conversation in an uncomfortable direction, I cut off communication.

By that time, I had met a really great guy, but we had only been on two dates when the calls started. Michael was very upset. He told me that I was damaged goods, and that he really wanted us to work out. I just ignored him.

A couple weeks later I was with my friend Bryanne at the local Walmart when I had the scare of my life. We were in the shoe section when we heard a man harassing a woman in the next aisle. We could hear her saying that she didn't need any help, but he blocked her from leaving. We stood listening, peering through the shoe racks ready to intervene. We heard the man shuffle out of the aisle and into ours.

It was Michael.

Bryanne knew all too well who he was and recognized him immediately from the pictures I had showed her. He knew that we were on this side of the aisle.

"Celina," he said. Bryanne grabbed my arm and pulled me out of the aisle.

We darted around Walmart, shocked that he was truly pursuing us. We dropped the items we were going to buy and ran for my car.

The Honda Civic that had been parked at my house and followed me around town was now parked against my driver's door.

I ripped open the passenger door and flew though to the other side before putting the car in gear and taking off. That night I told my parents. They were disappointed I'd kept secrets, but at the same time so happy that I finally told them. We decided to just ignore

Michael and hopefully, like a bee, he would go away.

The texts never stopped from Michael, but after that day I didn't see him again.

It wasn't until the distant future that I would hear of his name once more.

On April 8th 2009, our little town of Woodstock, Ontario was torn apart by two people from different places. A beautiful, bright 8-year-old girl named Victoria – Tori for short - went missing. She hadn't returned home after school. By that evening the town was covered in missing person posters and the whole city was drenched in the hopes that she was just playing at a friend's house and forgot the time.

My mom and I sat on the couch that night watching the news, biting our nails, and hoping for a positive report. Suddenly, I grabbed my mom's hand. I was having one of my "moments".

I saw from the hips down what Tori was reported wearing when she went missing. She was walking with a man and a woman downhill along a tree line. I reported this to my mom, but she said that it probably just my imagination because all that was going on.

A couple months later I woke in a panic without knowing why. I was supposed to work, but felt way too jittery to go. I called in and went for a walk, hoping to shake off whatever it was that I was feeling. As I re-entered the house an hour later, my mom called to me from the back living room, where I found her watching the news. She grimly announced, "Victoria is dead. They have her killer." My mouth, dry I stepped into the room and saw the image that was being shown on the news.

It was Michael.

I couldn't breathe. I ran as fast as I could, but only managed to reach the side of my house before I collapsed and began to vomit in the bush. The rest was a blur, but I spent countless hours over the next few weeks at the police department going over and over everything I knew about Michael, and I explained in detail how he had stalked me.

The police told me that Michael and his accomplice Terri Lynn had abducted Tori at 3.40pm, and she met the end of her beautiful life by 7 pm. According to my phone records, Michael had texted me twice that day: once that afternoon, and once in the late evening. The detectives wanted to know if I still had the messages, or if I remembered what they had been about. Unfortunately, I had carelessly left that phone on the city bus months before. All I could remember was that Michael had stopped texting me around the time of her disappearance.

To this day I live with so much anger and guilt. What if he had sent the message asking for me to meet him somewhere? If this was the case maybe I could have saved her. I was older, stronger. And honestly, I would take that spot of that little girl.

Our town changed that day. No one felt safe letting their kids go anywhere alone. Doors were always locked and everyone became suspicious. I changed, too. The guilt I carried was too much for me. I decided to apply as a last-minute decision to police foundations. If there was a way to save people, I needed to to play that role. My mistake was not taking the time to talk to someone about all the feelings I was dealing with. Everyone just told me there was nothing that I could have done, but I never believed that.

I started police foundations that September, but it all proved too much and I had to leave school. I would spend the next two years healing, finding myself, and living every day as vibrantly as possible for Tori.

In early January 2012 I got a call asking for me to testify against Michael Rafferty. I remember being in the kitchen and handing the phone to my mother because I couldn't hear the officer's voice over the sound of blood pounding through my ears.

That night I lay in bed with my eyes open just trying to figure out how a girl from the suburbs has lived this kind of life.

On the anniversary of Tori's disappearance, my friend Kaitlin and I gathered 300 purple balloons and the 350 purple butterflies that I'd made. We spent the entire night decorating the town in her honor. From her grave to her school, we lit the town up with her favourite color.

A couple months later I had the dream. I was in an arcade in Niagara Falls, Ontario. I had unlimited coins to play with whatever machine I wished - then Tori walked up beside me. We spent the night playing games and having the most amazing time. Once we got tired we sat at a table. She looked me straight in the eyes and told me that I wasn't allowed to feel the way that I was feeling. That she didn't even know what happened to her.

She never gave me any messages to pass on. When I asked her how she knew I was feeling like this, she said that she had found me in the thoughts of her family. I asked her to give me a sign that this was more then a dream, as I needed that to believe she was truly reaching out.

At 5.30 am I awoke from the dream shaking my head. I wanted more then anything for it to be a real visitation. I spent the next hour showering, eating breakfast, and waiting for a sign - nothing. At 6.30 am I stepped out of the door onto the front porch. I looked up as I unlocked my car. In the front yard laying haphazardly was one of the purple butterflies I had made months before.

THE SUMMONING

Somehow I found myself walking into a war zone. A paranormal group based out of Sarnia Ontario had called me after they had exhausted every other resource within 100 km in every direction. The paranormal team had spent countless nights and the founder had even moved into the house to help the family feel safer.

The past six months for the family had been one crazy event after another. Judy and Mike had taken in their first foster child nearly a year ago. They had so much luck raising their other two sons - now 14 and 17 - that they felt they should be responsible and help a child in need. That is where Brandon comes in. He had been bounced around various foster homes for years and the family had been warned he could be difficult, but they felt up to the challenge.

When Brandon arrived, he said his hellos and went to the room he was to share with the family's 17-year-old son, Jacob. Judy and Mike were a bit taken aback by the boy's black dyed hair, pants hung with chains, and tattoos that marred the 17-year-old boy's body.

From all aspects, Brandon was a kind boy, and his appearance didn't fit the stereotype that fell on young people who dress that particular way. He always went to class, did his homework, and even helped do dishes after dinner.

Judy and Mike felt they had lucked out, and even enjoyed Brandon's company. Many times Judy tried to be a mother figure and get close to Brandon; however, every time she asked a personal question or tried at all to be kind in the way only a mother can, he came up with some excuse of homework or needing to use the restroom. This broke Judy's heart. She knew that this alienation was because the poor boy had been passed around like the collection plate at church for most of his life.

They were two months in when Mike and Judy's youngest son Josh approached them with a strange story. He said he was in the garage working on his bike when Brandon came in with a black book and asked Josh if he wanted to hear a cool story. Brandon then proceeded to read dark lines from the black book. Once he was finished reading, he walked to Josh and asked if he wanted to be a part of a really cool club. Though only fourteen years old, Josh was smart for his age, and he laughed off the offer and turned away. When he turned for a wrench a few minutes later, he saw Brandon was standing in the same place. Brandon caught Josh's look and pulled a little Swiss Army knife from his jeans pocket, pulled the blade out, and pressed it into his palm. Josh was so shocked that he jumped backwards, falling over his bike. Brandon laughed and said it was that easy. That all he needed to do to join was to cut his hand, and shake hands. Josh bolted out of the garage and spent the rest of the night in his room deciding if he should tell his parents or just keep the weird moment to himself. While he hadn't been a fan of Brandon's from the start, Josh knew that Brandon was a good kid and didn't want something like this to make his parents decide he wasn't safe and ship him off like every other family did.

That night Josh was finishing up some homework on his laptop when he felt hands on his shoulder. He hadn't even heard Brandon come in the room. The hands started kneading into his shoulders, and Josh didn't move as he assessed what kind of rub this was, but it didn't feel innocent.

Josh could feel Brandon's breath right against his head, hot, wet and smelling of pot. "Are you sure you don't want to join my club?" Josh could feel the sly grin forming in Brandon's words. Josh backed up his chair hard into Brandon, knocking the wind out of him, and then sprang up and rushed down the stairs of the split-level. He tore into the living room with force. The whole situation had made him so angry. Tears were forming as he yelled everything Brandon had said and done. Josh had always been a very quiet boy, so when he had something to say his family, always listened.

Trying to keep an open mind, Mike called for Brandon to come downstairs. When the adults questioned Brandon, he denied everything. Josh became livid.

Mike and Judy didn't know what to do, so they left it alone for a few days, but Josh stuck to his story. They finally decided that it wasn't worth the upset of Josh to keep Brandon in the home. That night they made the call they never wanted to make.

The next day the social worker arrived and the family watched as Brandon ignored the family and went right into the car. Before the car pulled off he rolled down his window. "I'll miss you Joshy," he said, as he smiled and the car pulled away from the curb.

A week later, the family had a meeting and came to the conclusion that their fostering adventure was at an end. It wasn't worth the chance. They felt they had done all that they could for Brandon, but it wasn't enough. It is possible that Mike and Judy realized they didn't feel right fostering when they had such an impressionable 14-year-old in the house.

Along with the decision to end fostering came the dissecting of Jacob's room. They were removing the twin bed and desk from the left side of the wall. Jacob and Mike first started with the mattress when they noticed something on the wall; there was an assortment of symbols carved into the drywall. When they moved the box spring and the wooden captain's bed, they found the wall was decorated in the strange markings and symbols, the same length of the bed.

Judy sat against the wall and pressed her fingertips into the deep lines as Mike stirred the plastering mud that would soon fill them. Within a few days the spot on the wall matched the rest of the blue wall around it.

The first night, when the paint was barely dry, Jacob woke to the feeling of someone lowering themselves onto his bed. He strained his eyes in the night to see a large man standing at the end of his bed. Jacob reached for his bedside lamp, and as he looked back in the light that echoed throughout the room, he saw that the man was simply gone. He moved his eyes over the bed and saw that two large hoof-shaped prints were pressed into the green comforter. The prints were outlined in what looked like black ink.

Jacob screamed for his parents, who rushed into the room and saw the marks without seeing anything else. Judy was about to get mad at Jacob for ruining the blanket when she realized that the marks were in the shape of what looked to be a horse hoof. Jacob explained what he had seen, and his mother's mind went directly to the carvings she found in the wall.

Without her family's knowledge, she had taken a picture of the symbols and headed off to the library. The symbols were all connected to the Satanic bible, and a lot of them represented demons that you could summon. She was not afraid of what she found because as a teenager, she herself had been into all those kinds of things. She had dated a very eccentric guy who was convinced he was the devil's brother, so they and their friends spent many nights in the cemetery trying to contact the dead. Luckily, she had grown out of this dark phase. Unfortunately, her ex-boyfriend wasn't as lucky. He had messed with the wrong guys and found himself six-feet-under.

That night might not have scared Judy, but the slew of events that ravaged the family over the next few months did. It started with the hoofs, then the vulgar messages slurred against the ceiling. At first, the parents were worried Josh was lashing out and blaming the events on something or someone else. One night, the family sat in the living room as the family cat Marcus, a fat old tabby, was dragged backwards by its tail across the living room floor right in front of them. That wasn't all. Everything the family needed always went missing; if it was a razor, toothbrush, anything, it could always be found on the roof. The family had finally reached out to a local paranormal team when they awoke to find the stairway that connected the first floor to the second was gone. As if a backhoe had come in and torn it out. It was nowhere to be found.

At first, the paranormal investigators were unable to discover any evidence at all. As they were in the kitchen having a discussion about packing up and coming home, they heard a knock on the front door. The family had left the team alone for the night, so they didn't expect anyone to be at the door at 4:55 am. When they opened the door, they found all the camera equipment they had staged in various rooms around the house was now sprawled all over the front lawn. The interior lights of the three cars they arrived in were all on, lighting up the property like a Christmas tree.

Reviewing their footage, they found that all the cameras had shut off individually before being removed. The team then called in another team, who had an experience of their own. One woman found herself lost in the basement. She said she had passed though at least 200 doors before finally making her way upstairs. This was strange as the basement was one 20- by 30-foot room that contained only a single set of washing and drying machines.

One of the paranormal teams had heard of my name through a friend of mine and gave me a call. The day I arrived was stormy, and I needed to be quick. I made my way into the foyer but the family wasn't there. They had moved in with Mike's parents while the paranormal team sorted out what they thought was going on. They had also contacted a local church, but the pastor had not thought any of it and seemed annoyed by their claims.

I sat on the base of the stairs and tried to make a connection. No matter how hard I tried, I could not make the connection I was attempting.

The silver sparkles start to take over my vision, only to be pushed back out by inky blackness. I hold my breath and push harder. Like the pop of a bubble, my vision is gone. I feel for the banister beside me and hold on tight. I smell ozone and rotten eggs. I hear the sound of heavy, putrid breath and see an outline of something I can't quite describe. No matter how hard I try, I can't bring him into a complete focus. I start to get the dizzy feeling that one gets before passing out and I know I need to break the connection.

When I finally broke free, I awoke to discover I was on the front lawn of the house with the paranormal group all around me. I called to the lady closest to me to give me a paper and pen. I hurriedly drew from memory what I had seen before the image was gone forever. After viewing it, no one could make out the grotesque thing that I had drawn. I took a picture of the image and sent it directly to Pastor John at the local church. I knew that whatever was in that house needed more attention than anyone had expected.

I called the pastor that night, and he told me after a couple of hours brainstorming with some colleagues, he knew what the family was facing and had contacted the right people who would be able to help them.

Luckily, the group Pastor John had called were at the home the next day, and by midnight that night, they deemed the house free and clear and left for the night. They called the family back with the great news, and Mike and Judy thanked them over and over. They slept like rocks that night as the anxiety finally was leaving their minds. Around 10:30 the next morning after a celebratory breakfast, the family pulled onto their block, only to find it surrounded by fire trucks and police cars. That's when they learned that in the wee morning hours, their house had burned down almost to the ground.

A few days later the family sifted their way through the rubble that had once been their home full of memories. Now everything was black and ashen, not even the structure of the house itself recognizable. It was as if the slate had been wiped clean. The sharp, dark edges of burned framing might have looked menacing, but as soon as you touched the wood it would fall to ash as if the evil no longer had the power to stay strong. The family was heartbroken that their home was destroyed, but in the back of their minds they knew this meant they could start somewhere fresh and try to forget the horrors that had become their life.

It has been a few years since that night. I called to check in with the family when I decided to include their story in my book. Judy told me that since that night, good luck had filled their lives as if they had received a gift from the heavens after battling something so dark.

HOME SWEET HOME

My hometown was less than lush with opportunity when it came to buying my first house. By the age of 20, I had found myself a good-paying job, a handsome fiancé, and the means to, for lack of a better term, settle down. My fiancé was 26, and while we had never lived together, we opted to buy instead of rent and pay someone else's mortgage.

We were so lucky to have a fantastic real estate agent who took her time narrowing down the listings she thought would fit our lifestyle best. We were looking at roughly a dozen

homes in our price range of $140,000 and
$200,000.

I worried that embarking on a home-
buying adventure would not be as easy for me
as it would be for another prospect buyer, and I
was right. I found the quest incredibly tiring. So
many homes were full of the dense, raw energy
that follows a divorce. Worst of all, I would
enter a bedroom and get flickers of images in
my head of events that should never happen to
innocent children.

In all, we had gone through about fifteen
houses when we pulled up in front of a cute
three-bedroom 1950's bungalow. It was situated
on a slightly busy road, but the curb appeal was
exuberant. We pulled into the 90-foot driveway
and parked in front of the single car garage. We
made our way to the front door and walked into
a freshly painted, sparsely decorated home. The
kitchen and bathroom had been re-modeled but

the rich hardwood and crown moulding still remained.

As I walked the house, I saw nothing but splashes of color. Here and there, I picked up a thought, but as a whole, the home felt airy, free and like it should belong to us. We knew we had to have it, and the bidding war began.

The next morning at 9:30am, I walked out to the kitchen with a smile on my face and told my parents I had just bought a house.

The next few months flew by as we gathered all the items we needed for our new home. Before we knew it, the day had come and we were painting and moving our furniture into our first home. In addition to the rest of the house, we had to renovate the basement, which included laying down new wooden floors. It took nine coats of paint to cover the dark brown panelled walls.

Around the time I moved into this house was when I started to embrace the paranormal side of life. I finally put my real name out there, instead of operating under a pseudonym. I think that by moving out of my parents' house and truly feeling like an adult, I was finally able to see who I really was.

We moved into our home on August 31st, but it wasn't until January 14th that we had our first strange occurrence. As you know from the introduction, spirits have been known to find their way to me. Luckily, the spirits I mingled with never crossed the barrier of the physical doorway to my house. On January 14th we returned home from an afternoon shift. We opened our back door and headed down the stairs to the basement to take off our boots. At the bottom of the stairs, we were met with a foot of water. At first we didn't think anything of it, as the rain that poured from the skies that day affected many of the houses in our area. We simply called a contractor to dig up our home and seal the foundation, a step that ensured we wouldn't experience flooding again.

Unfortunately, all of the work that we did while renovating the basement was completely ruined, which required us to tear out the wood panelling and swollen wooden floors. During the tear down, we found a large red spiral behind the wall panelling that had shown its way through the layer of green paint that covered the block foundation. I placed my hand against the spiral to see if I felt anything odd. While I didn't, I kept that red spiral in the back of my mind.

Over the next few months the basement continued to flood, and it didn't stop. The water didn't seep through the walls or up from the floor, but seemed to come from everything in the basement. First, the washing machine overflowed when a cloth I had never seen before plugged the drain. Then the water softener began to leak. Again and again, the source of the water rotated between the washer and the softener, even after every precaution was taken. The water never stopped.

I knew that this was becoming more than bad luck. There was nothing threatening but I was surprised that whatever this was had come into a home I thought was free from the paranormal. I spent a lot of time trying to connect to whatever or whoever was using water as a channel of communication, but connected with nothing.

A month later I came home at 1am and was in my office going through emails when I heard mumbling. I paused for a moment to discern where the noise originated, and when I thought for sure it was coming from the slightly open window, I resumed my work. A few moments later I heard the sound again. This time, it didn't seem like it was coming from outside. I went slowly into the hallway and checked the thermostat to see if the heat had kicked on. However, it was glorious part of spring where it isn't too hot or cold, and the furnace had been off for days. Across from the thermostat was the cold air return. I sat beside the grate and heard the noise again. It was the sound of an upset, mumbling man, someone who might have even been crying. I sat in the dark and leaned down so my ear was closer to the vent.

The noise was louder, as if the man was right under the vent. As I tried to make out words from the muttering, my bedroom door seven feet away opened. My fiancé Adam, who was on days and had been asleep for at least 5 hours, was standing in the doorway looking at me sitting on the floor. "Were you crying?" he asked as he rubbed sleep from his tired eyes.

This was new for me. My "shared" experiences were far and few between. My fiancé was my polar opposite, an outdoors man who avoided anything creepy. I had to bribe him to go to a scary movie.

Quickly, I saw the realization cross his face as I shook my head slowly and pointed to the vent. I then pushed the same finger to my lips as if to say, "shhhhhh". Adam came over and listened. He, too, heard the man. Worried that someone was in the basement, he gripped me protectively. However, I knew that I had locked the door behind me when I came home and didn't think this was an intruder at all. Leaving me next to the vent, Adam quietly took to the basement with a bat, a light, and a whole bunch of courage. As I thought, he found no one in the house.

That night I slept restlessly. As I dreamed, I saw an upset young man around 25 years old pacing my basement. He stood 5'8 and had long brown curly hair and sported blue jeans and a black t-shirt imprinted with an abstract design. The only thing out of place was that he walked above the ground as if he was levitating.

The next morning I awoke super curious and contacted a local historian who was able to give me all the previous owners' names. I also questioned the neighbours, but I never found any information about the man. This led me to believe that somehow a spirit had made its way into my home.

After that night the flooding stopped, and I never saw the man again. It was as if he was simply passing through; a guest who stayed only for a couple of months.

My home has remained rather quiet except for a few instances of what I think are other spirits passing through. Every once in a while the house will have a cluster of days when the energy feels "off" and something happens. I was lucky to catch a couple instances on film. I have videos of a blender, a plate of butter, and a necklace holder making their way across the tops of furniture in my home.

It seems the more I work in the paranormal field, the more I become a beacon for the unknown. It's as if I am a lighthouse for the spirits, and they make their way to when they need to be seen or heard.

CASSIE

Imagine yourself walking blindfolded in a cornfield in the middle of February, trying to learn about where you and what's happening around you. That's about what it's like to try and learn everything in the world of the "paranormal". When it comes to parapsychology, demonology and everything in between, there are many professionals waiting and ready to tell you what's right, what's wrong, and how to conduct yourself when you come into certain situations. The truth, though, is that we're all walking around blindfolded, trying to figure out what we're doing.

You would think that the life I have lived would bring me to have an extremely deep belief in God. Truth be told, I don't know exactly what I believe in. A part of me certainly does believe in a higher power, as I have witnessed how a "man of the cloth" used verse to end a case of extreme demonic invasion. At the same time, I have also watched the overwhelming love of a sister perform the same act. Over the past decade I have been to countless conventions, met with many researchers, attended speeches, and read hundreds of books that discuss everything from demonology to parapsychology and what may lie in store for us.

All I know is that good and evil exists. I have seen it take many forms. Many different cultures call out to separate idols to help them when they find themselves in a dark place. I love the idea of something taking care of us and that we "go home" someday, but I feel that everyone should search out their own beliefs to find where they want to place their faith. I have spent so many years chasing people with questions you can only answer yourself. I know my ideas will continue to evolve. Every adventure I step into seems to make me look at the paranormal in a whole new light.

The following case showed me how dark things can really become. I still think of Cassie on the nights I lay awake. The fact is that sometimes doing your best won't always be the solution; sometimes people can't heal from the events they have lived through and the things they have seen.

By all accounts, Cassie was a vivacious and eccentric 8-year-old. An only child, her days were full of school, dance, swimming, and whatever the red-haired girl's heart desired. Her parents both worked full time at jobs that allowed them to live a very posh lifestyle.

It all began when her father was transferred from Florida to Ontario. At first, her parents Elianna and Ricardo were hesitant to uproot their daughter from the family and friends she cherished so deeply. However, after weeks of consideration, they felt she was young, open, and mature enough to handle a change of scenery. Within the month they bought a brand new home over the phone, shipped their belongings, and finally boarded the plane for snow-covered Ontario, Canada.

Cassie was enthralled when the plane touched down that January. She had never seen snow, and ran down the sidewalk catching snowflakes on her tongue as they waited for her father's company car to arrive.

After a 45-minute ride from the airport, they pulled up in front of a modern stucco house with a three-car garage. This was not Elianna's idea of "home," as she had grown up in a country house. She found comfort in faucets that didn't work, dirty walls, and zero neighbours. All these homes seemed to only be ten feet apart.

Inside the house was every modern amenity one could think of and more. There were four bedrooms, four bathrooms and more space than their family of three could ever need. Ricardo was captivated by their home. He had grown up poor, and now he was like a child exploring every nook and cranny. The movers had set up the house with their belongings a week before they arrived.

Cassie was obsessed with the new house. Their prior house had not been small, but was more of a dated home that was around thirty years old. This house was open concept, and the ceilings were barely visible to the young girl.

The first four months in the new home were nothing more than ordinary. Other than some unpacking, they felt at home within a week of the move. No one in the family thought they would love snow so much. Cassie settled into school and made a ton of new friends who envied the fact she had been to Disney World.

Once spring rolled around, the family hired a contractor to dig up the backyard to install an in-ground pool. It wasn't long after they cracked the ground that they discovered they weren't bringing up only dirt. The family were in the backyard watching the men work from the porch when the contractor yelled out for the men to halt. Cascading from the piles of dirt were endless amounts of bones.

A wretched stench came from the ground. The contractor jumped into the 4-foot-deep hole and saw that each side was littered with bone fragments. There were so many; too many. After an hour of deliberation and examination of some skulls, it was obvious that the bones were those of horses. It was also clear from the brittleness of the bones that they had been there for at least 100 years. As people discussed what was happening, there were more and more comments about how the smell of rot had disappeared as fast as it had consumed the entire yard. They found it strange that the whole gross experience only lasted a second. Bones that old shouldn't carry any smell whatsoever.

However, the men proceeded with their work, and by mid-summer the kidney-shaped pool was bright blue and full of cold, refreshing water to help the family combat the fiery Canadian summer.

It was a very hot day in August when Ricardo and Elianna sat by the pool and watched Cassie and her friend Samantha take turns running along the deck and jumping onto one of the assorted inflatable toys in the pool. Cassie jumped onto the oversized alligator and slid off the other side like she had many times before, only this time, her little red head didn't pop up. Worried, Ricardo raced to the edge of the pool to check on his daughter.

Cassie was in the deep end, standing on the bottom of the pool floor. It took Ricardo a moment to realize that this pose was impossible to maintain. He also found it strange that Cassie seemed to be waving at him, and motioned for her to come up for air. Cassie only started waving her hands more urgently. Ricardo felt the rush of panic and jumped in as fast as he could. His feet hit the bottom and he grabbed Cassie and pushed off the bottom of the pool, but his daughter wouldn't budge. It was as if the little girl's feet were glued to the bottom of the pool.

Ricardo frantically felt her feet and legs to see what was holding her to the bottom. There was nothing. Ricardo violently pulled on the little girl; her panicked arms were starting to slow. At that moment Elianna knew something was wrong, and she jumped in to grab Cassie and her husband.

She too felt the concrete stance of her daughter, but an instant later, Cassie's body released from the pool floor and the family shot to the surface. Cassie broke the water first, gasping hard for air. She never lost consciousness, but her eyes looked as if they were going to pop from her head. Ricardo pushed her hair back from her face and asked if she was okay. Cassie made eye contact, but didn't even move her lips to try and say a word. Exhausted, the family of three climbed out of the pool and collapsed in the grass, where they found Samantha crying in fear.

By that afternoon, Ricardo had the pool company draining the pool as he screamed at them about how his daughter had almost died. The company gave him their word they would find the problem - except the problem was that there *was* no problem. The place where Cassie had been stuck was free and clear of anything that could have restricted her. Ricardo examined the pool floor himself but found nothing. All the men could do was shake their heads in disbelief.

A week passed and Cassie still had not muttered a single word. They had been to the doctor and even tried to bribe her with a new iPad, to no avail. Daily, Cassie was becoming less responsive. The doctor thought maybe she had honestly had the words scared right out of her, that sometimes children stop talking as a coping mechanism. After a perfect MRI, the doctor suggested they keep Cassie on her regular routine. That quickly proved challenging, as the little girl who was once so vibrant and full of lustre became withdrawn and strange, and was completely unrecognisable from the girl she had become overnight.

When her mother woke her for school, Cassie would shut the blinds and crawl under her bed. Most days Elianna called into work and stayed home to stay with her daughter. On the days she did go to school, Elianna would receive calls from her teacher stating that Cassie had been doing very disturbing things in class, from drawing fields of dead animals to cutting off classmates' hair and hoarding it in her desk.

One night, Elianna and Ricardo bought Cassie a kitten. She had always wanted one. They hoped if she had a kitten to cuddle and care for, she might finally speak. They walked into the bedroom and held the kitten up for Cassie to see, and the little girl's eyes lit up as she smiled. This was the first smile they had seen in a month. Elianna and Ricardo were so happy with the progress that they handed her the kitten without her uttering a word.

The next morning, they awoke and made their way to Cassie's room to wake her for school. Elianna called out that it was time to rise and shine, and Cassie opened her eyes with a big smile on her face. Ricardo told her it was time to get up, but she didn't budge. He repeated himself, but she lay in the same spot with a big silly grin on her face. Finally, her mother came over and sat her up, then recoiled in horror. In the spot where Cassie had been laying was the kitten's lifeless body. Cassie had rolled right on top of it and laid there all night. As her parents backed away from the kitten, the smile never left Cassie's face. Elianna knew instinctively that Cassie had intentionally killed the kitten.

The gruesome smile remained on Cassie's face during breakfast, and her mother made an emergency appointment with the doctor's office. While she got dressed, her parents asked her questions and told her what she had done. Her obnoxious grin didn't fade until the doctor suggested Cassie spend a few nights in the hospital under observation. At this point, even her parents didn't fight the idea.

They were afraid for their daughter, and afraid of what she was capable of.

That night, in the house that felt too empty without their daughter, Elianna and Ricardo sat in their daughter's bedroom. They had taken the cat out back that morning and buried it in the rose garden. It was so sad to see the poor little orange kitten's life cut short so soon. They were talking about the idea of moving back home and being closer to family when the blinds in Cassie's room shot down in record speed, submerging the room into darkness. Thinking the blinds must be faulty, Elianna rose to her feet to raise them back up.

She was again mentioning how going home to Florida might be best for them when a doll fell from the top shelf of Cassie's closet. Ricardo was immediately on his feet, his eyes locked with Elianna's. She knew what he was about to do. Ricardo then loudly announced, "Yes, we are going to pack up and move within the week." As soon as the words left his mouth, the bedroom door slammed shut, as if by an angry teenager. Neither Elianna nor Ricardo even flinched, just held each other's gaze. The couple didn't acknowledge what had happened; Ricardo had grown up very superstitious, and his mother was considered a healer. He had told his wife time and time again that to acknowledge those things gave them power. Elianna was not about to question what she knew her husband was thinking, as she herself had seen some pretty strange things. In that moment, she questioned herself on why she hadn't considered earlier that more was going on than just a sick daughter.

Ricardo and Elianna went out for lunch to talk about what had happened. They opted for coffee as they were too nauseated by what they had witnessed to choke down any food. Ricardo first suggested that now that Cassie was in a hospital and away from the house, maybe

she would be fine. Elianna agreed. Ricardo
called his mother in Florida and asked her what
to do. They did not have a close relationship,
and they had barely spoken since they had
moved. However, after explaining the events of
the past few months – the bones, the near-
drowning, the cat - she suggested to start by
contacting Native groups in the area.

Over the weekend, Elianna and Ricardo
received a call from the hospital with the
opposite news they were expecting. Cassie had
gotten worse. While she was still not speaking,
she was now violently screaming and trying to
hurt herself. Elianna ran to be with her
daughter as Ricardo made some calls.

A few days later, Ricardo met with
someone who had been recommended to him
as a well-respected man from the Native
community. Before he even finished stepping
out of his car, the man was already spouting
information about the land. As Ricardo walked

him around the house, the man explained that the entire area and much of the city was originally Native land.

After a long tour and "testing" the ground, the man concluded that the house and surrounding land was part of a ritual area. The bones dug up during the pool installation would have been used in rituals of many kinds - some good, some bad, and some you don't speak of. He called two other men and asked them to come to the house, and the three performed a blessing of their culture and tried to speak to whatever was causing this family harm. Ricardo noticed that by the time the men left, the home seemed to feel lighter, and he called his wife with the news. By this time, Cassie had undergone many tests, including MRI's that showed deterioration in her brain, a kind usually only seen in very old patients.

Elianna spent a week with Cassie at the hospital before deciding to spend a night in her own bed. After a peaceful night, Elianna felt a flicker of hope for the future. She washed and dried some laundry and went into Cassie's room to put it away. As she pushed open the door, she felt something behind it, preventing her from opening it all the way. Sticking her head around the door, she found that all the toys in Cassie's room from the closet, boxes, and toy shelf were piled behind the door. Elianna collapsed.

Around this time I had put an ad up on Kijiji for "home reading" that explained what I did and how to contact me. I received the following message:

Dear Celina,

The past few months have been filled with tragedy. Things beyond our wildest fears have occurred and I don't know what our future holds. I don't care the price; we need to have some idea of what is happening.

Elliana & Ricardo
1-519-XXX-XXXX

With a message like that, I placed a call to them immediately and Elianna picked up. I could tell from the tone in her voice I needed to get there right away. I explained my process and told her I do not charge for my services. She asked how soon I could come by. Being that they were only a short two-hour drive from my home I set out that day.

I found the house located in a new, pretty suburb. I met Elianna at the door. I shook her hand and tried to hold eye contact with her, but her eyes were so sad and tired I could only hold her gaze and hand for a second before her energy overwhelmed me. I took a seat on the stairs next to the front door. I stared at a pebble in the space between two floorboards and focused.

I feel the wood slip away from me. The walls of the house become crystallized, like a shiny see-through mirror. I walk around the

*house but find it hard to concentrate, so I make
my way into a pink bedroom. It is the most
girlish room I have ever seen, but the pink walls
are not bright enough to cover the sick feelings
and the dark blue mist that engulfs the entire
ceiling. I feel drawn to the window and walk
towards it. Looking down, I see nine men and six
women of Native descent. Some are naked while
others are covered in hides. They all look
expectantly in my direction.*

 *I make my way downstairs and open the
crystalized backdoor. Now, only one woman
stands naked in the middle of the backyard. She
doesn't seem to notice me. Her feet are
submerged three feet into the ground, as if her
spirit isn't level with the lush green lawns that
now cover the property.*

 *The woman is breathing heavily. I walk
closer to her and hear her say, "He say I go." I
don't say a word, and after a moment she
repeats, "He say I go." With the blink of an eye,*

she's gone. I make my way to the porch and sit
down to regain normal reality.

I told Elianna what I had experienced, and she told me about everything: the horse bones, her daughter, the cat, the Native man and what he said. I suggested she contact him for me. Luckily, he wasn't busy and within the hour, two men and five women arrived at the house.

I sat with them and explained the group I'd seen from the window and the Native woman's words. Based on my information, the Native family was able to pinpoint the spirits they should try to contact.

The Elder man thought the spirits just needed some guidance. That night, Elianna, Ricardo and I left the house so that the group could conduct the rituals that they thought the house needed. The next day, the man met with

Cassie at the hospital. He said she was clear of the energy the house held.

After that day, all of Cassie's MRI's were absent of any sign of deterioration. She has shown a lot of progression since, but the truth is that she will never be the same girl she once was.

In this field of work, you see terrible things, but the feeling that comes when you witness the comfort you can restore to a family torn apart by the unknown is a beautiful thing. I don't think there is one person in this field who doesn't have a certain family or individual that haunts them more than any ghost.

There are good stories and there are bad stories.

My story is just getting started.